REAL CHRISTIANITY

REAL CHRISTIANITY
CONTRASTED WITH THE PREVAILING
RELIGIOUS SYSTEM

William Wilberforce

Abridged and Edited by James M. Houston

Introduction by Senator Mark O. Hatfield

MULTNOMAH PRESS
PORTLAND. OREGON 97266

This reproduction of William Wilberforce's work is based on the American edition of 1829, entitled *A Practical View of the Prevailing Religious System of Professed Christians, in the Higher and Middle Classes in This Country, Contrasted with Real Christianity.*

Scripture references in this volume are either directly quoted from the Authorized King James Version or are a paraphrase of that version by William Wilberforce.

Woodcut of William Wilberforce: Sarah Chamberlain

REAL CHRISTIANITY
This abridged edition
© 1982 by Multnomah Press
Portland, Oregon 97266

Printed in the United States of America

First Printing 1982

Library of Congress Cataloging in Publication Data

Wilberforce, William, 1759-1833.
    Real Christianity.

    "Based on the American edition of 1829 . . . A practical view of the prevailing religious system of professed Christians, in the higher and middle classes in this country"—P.
    1. Apologetics—18th century.   2. Christianity—Essence, genius, nature.
I. Houston, J. M. (James Macintosh), 1922-   II. Title.
BT1100.W52   1982   209'.033   82-8061
                                          AACR2
ISBN 0-930014-90-1

CONTENTS

PREFACE TO THE CLASSICS OF FAITH AND DEVOTION

With the profusion of books now being published, most Christian readers require some guidance for a basic collection of spiritual works that will remain life-long companions. This new series of Christian classics of devotion is being edited to provide just such a basic library for the home. Those selected may not all be commonly known today, but each has a central concern of relevance for the contemporary Christian.

Another goal for this collection of books is a reawakening. It is a reawakening to the spiritual thoughts and meditations of the forgotten centuries. Many Christians today have no sense of the past. If the Reformation is important to them, they jump from the apostolic Church to the sixteenth century, forgetting some fourteen centuries of the work of the Holy Spirit among many devoted to Christ. These classics will remove that gap, and enrich their readers by the faith and devotion of God's saints through all history.

And so we turn to the books, and to their purpose. Some books have changed the lives of their readers. Notice how Athanasius's *Life of Antony* affected Augustine or William Law's *A Serious Call to a Holy Life* influenced John Wesley. Others, such as Augustine's *Confessions* or Thomas à Kempis's *Imitation of Christ*, have remained perennial sources of inspiration throughout the ages. We sincerely hope those selected in this series will have a like effect on our readers.

Each one of the classics chosen for this series is deeply significant to a contemporary Christian leader. In some cases, the thoughts and reflections of the classic writer are mirrored in the leader's genuine ambitions and desires today, an unusual pairing of hearts and minds across the centuries. And thus these individuals have been asked to write the introduction on the book that has been so meaningful to his or her own life.

EDITING THE CLASSICS

Such classics of spiritual life have had their obstacles. Their original language, the archaic style of later editions, their length, the digressions, the allusions to by-gone cultures—all make the use of them discouraging to the modern reader. To reprint them (as was done on a massive scale in the last century and still so today) does not overcome these handicaps of style, length, and language. To seek the kernel and remove the husk, this series involves therefore the abridging, rewriting, and editing of each book. At the same time we sought to keep to the essential message given in the work, and to pursue as much as possible the original style of the author.

The principles of editing are as follows. Keep sentences short. Paragraphs are also shortened. Material is abridged where there are digressions or allusions made that are time-binding. Archaic words are altered. Spelling is that of Webster's Dictionary. Logical linkage may have to be added to abridged material. The identity of theme or argument is kept sharply in mind. Allusions to other authors are given brief explanation. And marginal readings are added to provide concise summaries of each major section.

For the Christian, the Bible is the basic text for spiritual reading. All other devotional reading is secondary and should never be a substitute for it. Therefore, the allusions to Scripture in these classics of devotion are searched out and referenced in the text. This is where other editions of these books may ignore the scriptural quality of these works, which are inspired and guided by the Bible. The biblical focus is always the hallmark of truly Christian spirituality.

PURPOSE FOR THE CLASSICS: SPIRITUAL READING

Since our sensate and impatient culture makes spiritual reading

strange and difficult for us, the reader should be cautioned to read
these books slowly, meditatively, and reflectively. One cannot
rush through them like a detective story. In place of novelty, they
focus on remembrance, reminding us of values that remain of eternal consequence. We may enjoy many new things, but values are
as old as God's creation.

The goal for the reader of these books is not to seek information. Instead, these volumes teach one about living wisely. That
takes obedience, submission of will, change of heart, and a tender,
docile spirit. When John the Baptist saw Jesus, he reacted, "He
must increase, and I must decrease." Likewise, spiritual reading
decreases our natural instincts, to allow His love to increase within us.

Nor are these books "how-to" kits or texts. They take us as we
are—that is, as persons, and not as functionaries. They guide us to
"be" authentic, and not necessarily help us to promote more professional activities. Such books require us to make time for their
slow digestion, space to let their thoughts enter into our hearts,
and discipline to let new insights "stick" and become part of our
Christian character.

James M. Houston

William Wilberforce
(1759-1833)

EDITOR'S NOTE ABOUT WILBERFORCE AND THE RELEVANCE OF THIS CLASSIC

THE BOOK

It is appropriate perhaps to the North American "born again" culture, today, to commence this classics series with William Wilberforce's manifesto; this is what he called his treatise on "Practical Christianity." The full title he gave it was "A Practical View of the Prevailing Religious System of Professed Christians, in the Higher and Middle Classes in this Country, Contrasted with Real Christianity." This reproduction has been based on the American edition of 1829 (reduced from 450 pages of small type in the earlier editions to 317 pages). The 1829 edition has now been further reduced but contains the book's central message.

The first five editions of the book were made in 1797. Ten years before, a worldly young politician, William Wilberforce, had been persuaded by a friend to read Philip Doddridge's *Rise and Progress of Religion in the Soul* (1745). Making a profound impression on him, it inspired him to write *A Practical View of . . . Real Christianity* as a result. His publisher was so doubtful of its success he only printed 500 copies. But in the same year five editions and some 7,500 copies had sold. Later it was translated into French, German, Italian, Spanish, and Dutch.

THE AUTHOR

The impact of this book on his society was immense, but its

greatest influence was on the author himself, since it found Wilberforce to be first a Christian, and then a politician. Entering Parliament at the age of twenty-one, Wilberforce became the close friend of William Pitt, the young Prime Minister of Britain. He could have succeeded Pitt in his political leadership, if he had "preferred party to mankind." But at the age of twenty-five, he became a committed Christian and henceforth he confessed that "God Almighty has put before me two great objects—the abolition of the slave trade and the reformation of the manners of England."

It was for this latter purpose that Wilberforce wrote this book. Among those who were profoundly influenced by it were people as diverse as the politician Edmund Burke and the agriculturalist Arthur Young. It may also be said that the publication of this book marked the beginning of serious concern for evangelical Christianity among the upper classes in England during the nineteenth century.

By the end of Wilberforce's life, there was no one more universally honored as an Englishman than he was. For the main credit for the abolition of the slave trade belongs to William Wilberforce. Behind that lay his consuming drive to manifest real Christianity.

THE MESSAGE TODAY

Today there is perhaps no one who more exemplifies the role of a true Christian in public service of government than Senator Mark Hatfield. John Newton exclaimed of Wilberforce's book, "such a book, by such a man, and at such a time!"

The endorsement of this work, at this time, by Senator Hatfield is also significant: He is a lay Christian safe from the imputation of professional bias. He is a politician, who also speaks responsibly of the major issues of our time. He is a consistent human being, who can say with Wilberforce, "How careful ought I to be, that I do not disgust men by the inconsistency between the picture of a Christian which I draw, and which I exhibit!"

We are deeply indebted to Senator Hatfield for his courage to endorse a book that changed the piety of England in the first half of the nineteenth century. We believe it needs recovery in our generation.

James M. Houston

INTRODUCTION

It is not uncommon for someone to be intrigued by a historical figure. But when you discern through reading his work and the work of his biographers that you have, in part, modeled your life after that person—this is an arresting experience. It is also, upon reflection, a deep encounter with the mysteries of the God who transcends time and nations.

This timely new edition of English Parliamentarian William Wilberforce's *A Practical View of . . . Real Christianity* is an invigorating supplement to the many articles and insights about him shared with me by friends. I have gained strength from the knowledge that there was one who had his life's personal and legislative agendas both exonerated by history and affirmed in the lives of individuals. To read Dr. James Houston's revision of this classic is an encounter with the biblical truth of "going from strength to strength" (Psalm 84:7).

A Practical View of . . . Real Christianity inspired a deep reevaluation of my own career: it led me to much-needed reflection, and it brought encouragement to my heart. Great understanding is shown in the lessons delineated by the founder of the Clapham Society regarding obedience, humility, family love, legislative priorities, and numerous other areas of concern for the follower of Jesus Christ. Two hundred years later his insights are a beacon for biblical faith and action.

In that wonderful passage in the prologue of John's Gospel, we have clarified for us and for all time past and future that the Word of Genesis became flesh and lived with us, full of grace and truth. There is this great light that has never been darkened, Who lit the way for those whose hearts were bound together in Clapham, England, and Who has blazed His track through the twilights of cultures and civilizations, even to our own day. This shaft of light gives us hope that in fact God became a man and humbled Himself so we could not only know Him personally, but have our lives transformed and made viable for His purposes. And the good news is that all of creation will one day be transformed into the new heaven and the new earth.

As we stand in this bright light that transcends the centuries and links our hearts to our parliamentarian brother, one of the most compelling and encouraging characteristics I find in Wilberforce's life was the resolve, early in his career, to focus legislative and personal agenda on building relationships. This took the place of power manipulation and legal machinations. In other words, he sought to continue the incarnation of the Word in loving acts of mercy, justice, and charity to those around him, even if they were adversaries.

It became my conviction early in my political life, at approximately the same age that it came to Wilberforce, that relational politics was essential if I was to be true to my seminal biblical convictions. People who became my closest spiritual friends when I was teaching at Willamette University, chiefly Doug Coe, then the Young Life Director in Salem, Oregon, taught me the sturdy nature of relationships that transcend differences. They were the incarnation who, like the hound of heaven, pursued me relentlessly down the highways and byways of my spiritual search.

My students heard from me that they should know with certainty what their political philosophy was so they could be intelligent in taking positions, rather than be faced with the awful prospect of abandoning their mind to others. When Doug Coe asked me in like manner what my religious convictions were based upon, I was struck by my own religious paucity and absences of commitment to the Lordship of Jesus Christ. Not only did this culminate in my own personal rededication, but I was inspired to relational faith that pointed to relational politics. The value of persons and the building of brotherly friendships became more important to me than the litmus test of ideological purity.

William Wilberforce's conversion came in debate over the presuppositions about the message of Christ. In his travels, Wilberforce discovered Isaac Milner, a tutor at Queens College. They read to each other for hours from the classics and the Bible, and spent an equal amount of time discussing what was read. His sons described in their biography of their father, *The Life of William Wilberforce*, the change in thinking that took place as he debated Milner. "I imbibed his sentiments, though I must confess with shame, that they long remained merely as opinions assented to by my understanding, but not influencing my heart. My interest in them certainly increased, and at length I began to be impressed with a sense of their importance."[1]

He later testified that "often while in the full enjoyment of all this world could bestow, my conscience told me that, in the true sense of the word, I was not a Christian." Just as Wilberforce had grown up in a home in which Jesus Christ was honored, I, too, had parents who nurtured me in the church and with Bible reading. But the Lordship of Christ was not compelling for me while I was distracted with the enchantments of the single life of a Navy man during World War II.

The sporting and social life became less attractive when Wilberforce was deeply touched through the ministry of John Newton, the former slaveship captain and composer of "Amazing Grace," who tutored him after his conversion. He helped him to memorize Scripture and directed him toward prodigious study. And, as important, informed him of the diabolical nature of the slave trade.

This was the genesis of Wilberforce's concern for the poor and for the enslaved. It shaped his entire political career. His personal life was shaped as well, and he became a deeply committed family man toward his wife, Barbara, and their six children. His affection for them was particularly evident in his correspondence, which included a common theme of the love of Christ who watched over them. In one such letter to Samuel, Wilberforce wrote: "Oh, my dear Samuel, I love you most affectionately, and I wish you could see how earnestly I long hereafter . . . to witness my dearest boy's progress into professional life, that of a growing Christian shining more and more."[2]

Certainly his family and political disciplines had a remarkable impact that all of us who serve desire to leave as a legacy much more than in any legislation. Well-known Wilberforce biographer John Pollock points out that, although he himself would probably have disagreed, evidence can be given that Wilberforce did much to spread his faith in Britain and abroad, as well as to create a

spiritual and moral climate that would affect succeeding generations.[3]

The very fact that Wilberforce has been rediscovered two centuries after his commitment to Christ and to the cause of justice is
a sign and seal that ideas are mere illusions until they take on the
form of a living and loving person. The central recurring message
of God's redemptive work in Jesus Christ is that each person's faith
in action can mature by the grace of God into a vibrant witness.
What I am hoping for in Dr. Houston's new edition of Wilberforce's manifesto is an extension of that vision. The Word which
became flesh goes on being written, not with pen and paper, but in
each human heart.

In other words, the definitive Word in Jesus Christ has a con-
tinuing expression reflected in each believer's words and deeds.
Christ lived out his life through William Wilberforce, and He does
today through each of us, whether in unnoticed work in shops,
homes, and factories, or in public life, offices, and schools. No one
has captured this truth more succinctly than author George Eliot
in her novel, *Janet's Repentance*. One of the main characters, Mr.
Tryan, points out to Janet Dempster that "God is training us for
the eternal enjoyment of his love." It is then that the author observes:

> Blessed influence of one true loving human's soul on
> another! . . . mysterious, effectual, mighty as the hidden pro-
> cess by which the tiny seed is quickened, and bursts forth
> into tall stem and broad leaf, in glowing tasseled flower.
> Ideas are often poor ghosts: they pass athwart us in thin
> vapor, and cannot make themselves felt. But sometimes they
> are made flesh; they breathe upon us with warm breath, they
> touch us with soft responsive hands, they look at us with sad
> sincere eyes, and speak to us in appealing tones; they are
> clothed in a living human soul, with all its conflicts, its faith,
> and its love. Then their presence is a power, then they shake
> us like a passion.[4]

There is no question in the mind of any objective student of history that William Wilberforce was such a powerful presence. His
influence continues to be incalculable, and I personally believe
that his example during this time of deep need in our national life
will be broadened considerably by this new edition of A *Practical*

View of the Prevailing Religious System of Professed Christians, in the Higher and Middle Classes in this Country, Contrasted with Real Christianity.

It is appropriate to examine briefly the faith of William Wilberforce that gave power to his witness. After his conversion through the influence of Isaac Milner in 1784, Wilberforce returned to Parliament in the winter of 1785, having reached a point of intellectual assent to the historic church doctrines of the biblical view of humanity, God, and Jesus Christ. Like many of us who became followers of Christ in our adult lives while pursuing political careers, Wilberforce suppressed these matters and pursued his political goals. I remember clearly in my own early days of faith the sometimes excruciating struggle as I sought to determine how much I should share my experience. This concern grew in part out of a deep desire not to manipulate or exploit people with my love of Jesus Christ. But I have to be candid, too, and admit that I was hesitant to make a public statement.

I remember the first time I named the name of Christ from a public platform. It was at a Young Life dinner in Salem, Oregon. The ballroom had mirrored pillars throughout, and I will never forget when I finally mustered the courage to name the Name beyond all names, it seemed to reverberate off each pillar, and I was suddenly struck with a most painful headache. In part, the first public witness was a sign to me not only that my life was on the line, that I was willing to be counted, but also of the futility and selfishness of life lived outside of Christ.

The battlelines were drawn, and struggle intensified. By the fall of 1785, the young Parliamentarian Wilberforce had entered a deep period of anguish. He rose each morning to pray and reflect upon his place as a human creature before a just God. Placing oneself completely in obedience to his Creator and Lord could possibly mean ostracism and loss of political popularity. Many of us have had to wrestle with the temptation to want both popularity and service to God. The resulting inner turmoil was great for him.

His period of "great change," as he later described it, compelled Wilberforce to seek out the counsel of John Newton. It was Newton who calmed Wilberforce's fears and restrained him from the temptation to retreat from public life. Writing to Wilberforce on December 7, 1785, Newton shared the following insight: "It is hoped and believed that the Lord has raised you up to the good of

His church and for the good of the nation."[5]

Wilberforce researcher Richard L. Gathro points out in an unpublished masters thesis that Wilberforce's intellectual progress to the truths of the Gospel gradually then became heart assent. This included the submission of his goals to the service of God and humanity. From that time forward, he lived a life of personal piety and discipline.[6]

Wilberforce's practical spiritual disciplines not only undergirded him, but provided a striking witness (along with other Christian models throughout the centuries) of the power resulting from faithful prayer, meditation, and Bible reading. This was a practice from which Wilberforce was seldom to deviate. Further, he submitted himself to a personal accountability relationship with Isaac Milner regarding the conduct of their lives. And as well, for his benefit and for that of the entire church in the years to come, he kept a spiritual journal. John Pollock points out that this private record was used by Wilberforce to assess his conduct and included the evaluation of eating habits, purity in relationships with women, and whether or not a check on ambition was being maintained. It is important to note that this inner severity was to be linked with a spirit of joy, which he believed to be a mark of the disciple of Jesus Christ.

The vibrant faith that resulted from his spiritual disciplines and secure family life gave him an evangelist's heart of concern for people of all backgrounds. He was ecumenical to the point of gathering a religiously mixed group of colleagues and the influential of the country for his causes in the Parliament. Many church-related projects were inaugurated, both at home and abroad, by this circle. These included some of the first foreign missionary efforts and concerted endeavors toward Bible distribution. Many church-related societies received generous financial support from the Wilberforce family, and William's name appeared on many advisory committees. In keeping with the inclusive spirit which developed out of his biblical faith, he spawned efforts to free Roman Catholics from religious and political oppression. One of his deepest desires was to encourage all Christians to love one another after the biblical imperative.

It was this growing circle of Christian brothers and sisters who encouraged him to write a "manifesto," although Dr. Milner sought to dissuade him. Books of this nature generally sold poorly as Dr. Houston points out in his Note on Wilberforce. The publishers hinted at this apprehension. But the book was an immediate success without precedent. By 1826, fifteen editions had been printed in Britain and twenty-five in the United States.

As with the personal writing of any public figure, Wilberforce's book provided his contemporaries with a comprehensive statement of his philosophy of life. I have in my home a bookshelf given strictly to a collection of books by my political colleagues. In addition to the joy of having personally inscribed copies of each of their political philosophies, I have a shelf full of windows into the souls of some of the men and women whom I have grown to love and respect over the years of my public life.

Many bridges for conversation and deep sharing are provided in reading the works of my contemporaries. This certainly was true of Wilberforce. One can never know for sure from the historical record, but I would venture from my own experience that Wilberforce's opportunities to discuss the Christian doctrines with many in the political life of England had a far-reaching impact into many homes and political decisions. " 'I heartily thank you for your book,' enthused Lord Manchester. 'As a friend I thank you for it; as a man I doubly thank you; but as a member of the Christian world, I render you all gratitude and acknowledgement. I thought I knew you well but I know you better now.' "[7]

Wilberforce emphasized in his writing the natural state of humanity as being apostate, fallen from the original creation, degraded and depraved, disposed to evil, and vile to the core. In Chapter 3, there is as clear a statement about the necessity of the atonement of Jesus Christ and the ministry of the Holy Spirit, as there is in the English language. His exposition of these doctrines is replete with Scriptures familiar to the evangelical Christian.

He understood that many people in cultures surrounded by the influence of the church make intellectual agreement to doctrines without realizing the personal significance, especially as it involves conviction of sin. He commented upon humility, conduct, and temperament, and warned the affluent about the dangers of falling prey to the "pomp and vanities of this world." He placed a strong emphasis on the life lived modestly. What a needed message in an age when our affluence is being found inadequate for our deepest needs!

When reading this book, as well as excerpts from his letters and journals, one is left with little doubt concerning the vibrancy of Wilberforce's faith. It was a faith with a high view of Scripture and specific applications to daily life. It was a faith that provided the strength to endure the challenges of life. It was a faith that provided particular strength to endure the challenges of the rough and tumble of political life. When he was in public disfavor for his support of the Sedition Bills in 1795, his journal entry reflected the biblical truth that "all things work together for good" and that the Lord protected him in specific ways from his political opponents.

William Wilberforce's faithful private spiritual life led to an exemplary public life. He served in the House of Commons from 1780 to 1825. When he first entered Parliament on October 31, 1780, he entered with a victory in which he amassed more than twice as many votes as his two opponents combined. He chose to sit with the Tory side of the House, along with his friend, William Pitt, in opposition to the party in power, the Whigs.

There is little doubt that in his early years, the primary motivation for Wilberforce was prestige and position. His political views were vague except for a sense of patriotism. He often followed Pitt's leadership. Even so, he declared himself a political independent quite early in his career, even while he felt particular loyalty to some of the Tory leaders. This, however, did not prohibit him from voting aginst the Tories on a number of issues, including Roman Catholic emancipation in Ireland and refusal to overreact to the French Revolution.[8]

He was always a proponent of parliamentary reform, regardless of sponsoring party. The abolition of the sale of parliamentary seats in 1809 was a further issue in which his position grew out of his personal conviction, and he was a significant source of assistance to the Prime Minister. But Wilberforce found himself most independent of the Tories on foreign affairs issues. He supported the Greeks in their war for independence, and during the political tensions with France, his words of restraint brought him the ire of the King, his friend Pitt, and his constituents. In fact, he became a temporary political exile over the French issue. It was only after Prime Minister Pitt had time to reflect on the integrity of his friend that their relationship was reestablished.[9]

Further, Wilberforce opposed hostile actions toward Ireland, believing that Roman Catholics should be won over by persuasion, rather than by arms. An indication of his persistence in his convictions about the use of force is that he even opposed hostile action with other countries when the issue involved the abolition of slavery.

I can speak very personally about the price that a politician pays when he opposes his country's policies in crucial foreign affairs matters. Through the years I have sought to base my political decisions on biblical principles of reconciliation, stewardship, and justice in the midst of issues such as the Vietnam War, human rights questions, military involvement, the nuclear arms race, and production of binary nerve weapons. The undergirding power of the Holy Spirit has been evident during all this time, even when one found himself on the enemies list at the White House.

Just as Wilberforce discovered that foreign policy differences with administrations led to domestic policy conflicts as well, I discovered early that massive military investments lead to crippled infrastructure in the crucial areas of education, health care, and agriculture development. We live in a world where only $260 per student per year is spent to educate our young, while on the average, $16,000 each year is expended to train one soldier. My opposition to the fact that we are pounding our plowshares into swords puts me often in the minority against administrations of both parties. My great political hero of this century, the classic conservative, Robert Taft of Ohio, spoke to this reality when he stated in 1951:

> No nation can be constantly prepared to undertake a full-scale war at any moment and still hope to maintain any of the other purposes in which people are interested and for which nations are founded. In short, there is a definite limit to what government can spend in time of peace and still maintain a free economy, without inflation and with at least some elements of progress in standards of living and in education, welfare, housing, health, and other activities in which people are vitally interested.

Experiences of political conflict cause one to mature in faith, and inevitably to become more independent in thinking. Wilberforce was one of those rare politicians in his day, or any day, who was willing to vote against the prevailing tide in order to follow his conscience and risk defeat by an obdurate constituency.

Wilberforce has been a great encouragement to me in this area.

He learned that even when he put himself in stark disagreement with his constituency, he could still prevail politically by making himself available to them. I have discovered time and again that when I take a position contrary to the voters, if I will say to them in all honesty that it is a matter of my personal conviction and then explain why, even if they continue to disagree with me, there will be growing mutual respect. I have found it not only a necessity, but a nurturing experience for me, to return to Oregon for a regular monthly swing trip for four or five days of facing the voters. Further, after Wilberforce's model, I seek to do my best, and instruct my staff to do likewise, to focus on particular areas that concern my constituents. In a difficult time economically, this resolve includes not only economic reform legislation, but also highest priority focus on response to constituent inquiries and care in the pursuit of three or four hundred veterans', Social Security, and Medicare cases each week. In focusing on similar issues in his day, Wilberforce found he as a politician could live out the Gospel in the practical way.

If Christians in political life cannot be witnesses in this most basic manifestation of the living Word on a day-to-day basis, then the whole concept of public service is a mockery. Of course, I often fail in this area. But it is a deep desire of my heart to be a reflection, however pale, of the Incarnate One who encountered the destitute widow of Nain in her need and who fed the hungry multitudes. It has become increasingly obvious to me that Christians reaching out in deed as well as word to touch the lives of the poor, the oppressed, the lonely, and the frightened, are the only expression in the flesh of the living Christ that many people are going to know. Wilberforce was certain, as I am, that social progress, if it is to be true, needs a biblical base.

In Chapter 6 of *Real Christianity*, Wilberforce outlines his presuppositions about public policy. The most perceptive to me is his belief about what a Christian view of government and the responsibility of the citizens to the state should be. He was unalterably convinced that the Christian faith had direct relationship to the activities of the state. The servant nature of our faith is found no more clearly than in his statement that "religion has generally tended to promote the temporal welfare of political communities." He even goes so far as to observe that "we must acknowledge that many of the good effects which true religion produces in political societies would be produced even by a false religion—if the false religion prescribed to good morals and upheld them effectively."

But he was convinced that true Christianity was peculiarly and powerfully adapted "to promote the preservation and health of political communities" which are undone by what he called their "grand malady." Only with the model and teachings of Jesus Christ could this dreadful disease of selfishness be healed in all its different forms in various societies and classes.

In the great and the wealthy, it displays itself in luxury, pomp, and parade, and in all the frivolities of a sick and depraved imagination. Such imagination seeks in vain for its own gratification, and is dead to the generous and energetic pursuit of an enlarged heart. In the lower classes, where it is not immobile under the weight of despotism, it manifests itself in pride and insubordination.

But in understanding the opposite of selfishness he did not spend a great deal of energy criticizing the poor and lower classes. His major indictment was against the frivolous wealthy and their depraved imagination. He knew that vital faith in its persistent practice would produce caring and healing among all classes of society.

When a people is conforming its corporate heart to the heart of Jesus Christ, deep caring which results in sensitive institutions, laws, and civil order are the final beautiful gifts. Wilberforce believed that vital Christian faith "does not favor that vehement and inordinate ardor in the pursuit of temporal objects, which progresses toward acquisition of immense wealth, or of widely spread renown. Real Christianity does not propose to gratify the extravagant views of those mistakenly politicians whose chief concern for their country is extended domination, the command of power, and unrivaled affluence." Today, as then, those who rule are meant to rule with meekness. To be in a position of civil authority is to take seriously the obligations to and the cares of those we serve.

The city of Washington in general, and the Senate in particular, are sources of tremendous temptation. The ego is massaged, importance is amplified, and all of the accouterments of power are made manifest. The elevator which goes to the Senate floor to vote is equipped with a button for senators and a button for the public. My push of the senators' button countermands the button pushed by an unaware non-senator on the elevator, and the elevator reverses to serve me first. When visiting a college campus or business establishment for a speech, I am treated with great deference, to the point that I wonder if persons, even Christian brothers and sisters, can relate to me as an individual with human and spiritual needs. The bombardment of station and status is so persistent that I must remind myself when home that my wife and children are not Senate staff people.

For Wilberforce, the civil order in a country resulting from the benevolence of vibrant personal and corporate faith would be a model for other nations. The integrity of a nation that deals with a selfless attitude would inspire confidence, dispelling the inquiries that were derived from jealousy and mistrust. Further, it was plain to him that biblical faith was the enemy of the self-aggrandizing patriotism that leads to the use of force rather than diplomacy. How many times have we all wondered in the numerous post-World War II hostilities such as Vietnam, the Yom Kippur War, and the Falkland/Malvinas conflict what would have made the difference between death-dealing military action and a mere respectful conversation to settle disputes.

I am increasingly convinced the longer I am in public life that the Founding Fathers of the American experiment had no intention whatsoever of separating vibrant faith from impact upon public policy. They did not mean that personal spiritual insights should be left outside the door of public policy debate. The First Amendment, with its towering insight about the government not being the establishing factor for religion, means merely that we are a pluralistic society. Thus the power of the federal bureaucracy should not be mobilized for any one denomination, sect, cult, or religion. This does not mean that secularism should prevail. Pluralism, not secularism, was their intention. We are desperate for the insights of all people of faith in our national life.

I have been impressed so often with St. Paul's teaching in Corinthians that the eye cannot say to the hand, I have no need of thee. "We all see through a glass darkly." The insights of all are necessary for the survival of our common order. This is why it is so offensive to see religious pressure groups who in a self-anointed way are announcing to the community who is "most Christian" and what are the absolute "right" positions on public issues.

Wilberforce believed that the English Constitution, as well, provided for such a model society. Therefore, it was the responsibility of those in authority to have as central to their purpose, not only personal morality beyond repute, but also care in the legislating of the common order "and any plans which may be formed for the advancement of morality."

Certainly, abolition is the issue which gives us the greatest insight into his unflagging desire to have personal spiritual convictions borne out in the body politic at large. We have seen that the genesis of Wilberforce's thinking began with the tutelage of John Newton.

There were others, certainly, who brought this issue before him. He read and studied diligently and concluded that something had to be done about this "wickedness." But it was William Pitt who was reputed to have said: "Wilberforce, why don't you give notice of emotion on the subject of a slave trade? You have already taken great pains to collect evidence, and are therefore fully entitled to the credit which doing so will ensure you. Do not lose time, or the ground may be occupied by another."[10]

Along with the abolition of slavery, he was convinced that the moral condition had to be improved in England. And it was after he recorded in his diary in October of 1787 these two great objectives, "the abolition of the slave trade and the reformation of manners," that he began to depend increasingly upon an intimate group of friends to undergird him. Deterrence of the great evil was not sufficient, but a deep reformation of personal morals was needed as well. So without any elaborate organizational base, the Clapham Sect was born with two main points of commonality: their serious piety as followers of Jesus Christ and their philanthropy.[11]

If there is an area in Wilberforce's life and theology that should be held up to closer scrutiny, it was his views concerning the future and certain issues confronting his nation and his world. In his view, the end of a society of classes would come only with the second coming of Christ, not with a manifestation of the kingdom on earth. The great areas of biblical justice were left largely untouched by the Clapham Society . . . that God is a God who exercises his justice on earth (Jeremiah 9:24).

However, it must be pointed out that contact between different segments of society in that era was minimal. The agrarian social structure prevented the upper class from knowing the extent of the social evils around them in the cities. It is necessary that we realize our suburban/urban emotional separation is not that different today. We could easily stand under the same judgment by future historians if we cannot learn to bridge the gulf between the suburban affluent and the urban and rural poor.

As we look square in the face of immense poverty and starvation across our world (21 children are dying each minute), and in the face of more than 50 million abortions worldwide a year, and at the hideous cloud of nuclear war hanging over us which could end life on this planet, it is distinctly possible that we must—for our very survival—embrace again the well-delineated essentials for national repentance and reformation. The patience and persistence and love for detractors with which Wilberforce and his Clapham Society took on and then abolished the slave trade in 1807, and ultimately accomplished complete emancipation in 1833, stands as a great beacon light to those of us today who are involved in the entire scope of "Pro-Life" issues. I am persuaded that the parallel issue in the twentieth century to slavery in the nineteenth is this very cluster of issues that flow from our present-day manifestation of the "grand malady": selfishness.

How is it that we dare commit the sin of the ultimate idolatry in seeking to rob the Creator of His creation? (The sin of a lack of love for adversaries was, in Wilberforce's view, just as wrong as being incorrect on an issue. We must face this in our own era of history. We must come to grips with this side of the sinful spirit.) Only focus on self to the exclusion of all others could possibly bring us to this disobedience.

It is not inconceivable to believe that under the guidance of the Holy Spirit and with the use of political acumen, such severe anti-life tensions could be reduced and then abolished just as slavery was abolished worldwide. Just as there was no ultimate economic security in owning slaves, there is no ultimate political security in owning weapons that destroy not only those who receive the blow, but those who give it. Further, it is not revisionist history to assert that the secondary goal of improved "manners" flows naturally from the deep repentance that came from abolition.

How I pray that in our lifetime we might abolish the fear and malappropriation of resources that we now experience. It is entirely possible, even probable, that this vision will not be accomplished as easily as was Wilberforce's. But we are promised, as people of the kingdom of God, that our faithfulness will play a part in the consummation of all history. We are promised that there will be a new heaven and a new earth.

William Wilberforce's pinnacle contribution was to give us confidence of the assurance that "Thy kingdom come on earth as it is in heaven" is a reality worth trusting.

Senator Mark O. Hatfield

---

[1]Robert Isaac and Samuel Wilberforce, *The Life of William Wilberforce* (Philadelphia: Henry Perkins, 1839), pp. 87-88.

[2]Anna Maria Wilberforce, *The Private Papers of William Wilberforce* (New York: Burt Franklin, 1897), p. 165.

[3]John Pollock, *Wilberforce* (New York: St. Martin's Press, 1977), p. 105.

[4]George Eliot, *Scenes of Clerical Life*, vol. 2: *Janet's Repentance* (1858, reprint ed., New York: Garland Publications, Inc., 1975), pp. 284-85.

[5]Pollock, *Wilberforce*, p. 38.

[6]Mr. Gathro's study, entitled *William Wilberforce and Integration of Faith with Public Policy*, written for Wesley Theological Seminary, was an enormous help to me in organizing my thoughts for this introduction.

[7]Samuel Wilberforce, *Life of Wilberforce* (London: J. Murray, Publisher, 1868), p. 169.

[8]Sir Reginald Coupland, *Wilberforce, A Narrative* (Oxford: Clarendon Press, 1923), p. 353.

[9]Oliver Warner, *William Wilberforce and His Times* (London: B.T. Batsford, Ltd., 1962), p. 156.

[10]Pollock, *Wilberforce*, p. 58.

[11]Francis John McConnell, *Evangelicals, Revolutionaries and Idealists* (New York: Abingdon-Cokesbury Press, 1942), pp. 158-63.

I

INADEQUATE CONCEPTIONS OF THE
IMPORTANCE OF CHRISTIANITY

t is proper at this time to point out the very inadequate conception which professing Christians entertain of the importance, nature, and superior excellence of Christianity. If we listen to their conversation, virtue is praised, and vice is censured. Piety is perhaps applauded and profanity condemned.

So far all is well. But let anyone who is not deceived by these barren generalities examine these Christians' profession a little closer. He will find they do not pay homage to Christianity in particular. At best they pay homage to religion in general—perhaps to mere morality.

With Christianity, professing Christians are little acquainted. Their views of Christianity have been so cursory and superficial that they have little more than perceived those exterior circumstances which distinguish it from other forms of religion. These circumstances are some few facts, and perhaps some leading doctrines and principles, of which they cannot be wholly ignorant. But of the consequences, relations, and practical uses of these principles, they have few ideas—or none at all.

Does the language seem too strong in speaking of professing Christians? View their plan of life and their ordinary conduct. Wherein can we discern the points of difference between them and acknowledged unbelievers? In

How inconsistent we are in Christian education compared with education in the world.

1

an age in which infidelity abounds, do we observe them carefully instructing their children in the principles of faith which they profess? Or do they furnish their children with arguments for the defense of that faith?

They would blush on their child's birth to think him inadequate in any branch of knowledge or any skill pertaining to his station in life. He cultivates these skills with becoming diligence. But he is left to collect his religion as he may. The study of Christianity has formed no part of his education. His attachment to it—where any attachment to it exists at all—is too often not the preference of sober reason and conviction. Instead his attachment to Christianity is merely the result of early and groundless prepossession. He was born in a Christian country, so of course he is a Christian. His father was a member of the Church of England, so that is why he is, too.

When religion is handed down among us by hereditary succession, it is not surprising to find youth of sense and spirit beginning to question the truth of the system in which they were brought up. And it is not surprising to see them abandon a position which they are unable to defend. Knowing Christianity chiefly by its difficulties and the impossibilities falsely imputed to it, they fall perhaps into the company of unbelievers.

Let us therefore beware before it is too late. Let us beware that, in schools and colleges, Christianity is almost—if not altogether—neglected. We cannot expect those who pay so little regard to this great object of education of their children to be more attentive to it in other parts of their children's conduct. If they have little regard for the state of Christianity, they will be still more indifferent about communicating the light of divine truth to the nations which "still sit in darkness."

But is not Christianity a private affair!

But religion, one may reply, is not noisy and ostentatious. It is modest and private in its nature. It resides in a man's bosom, and shuns the observation of the multitude. Be it so.

From our transient and distant view of these unassuming Christians, let us approach a little nearer, and listen to the unreserved conversation of their confidential hours. Here, if anywhere, one sees the interior of the heart laid open. And we may ascertain the true principles of their affections and aversions; the scale by which they measure the good and the evil of life.

Here, however, you will discover few or no traces of Christianity. It scarcely finds a place amidst the many objects of their hopes and fears, their joys and sorrows. They are grateful perhaps, as well indeed they may be grateful for health and talents, affluence, and other temporal possessions. Yet they scarcely reckon this grand distinguishing mark of the bounty of God's providence among their many blessings. Or if they mention Christianity at all, they notice it coldly and formally. We could liken this act of mentioning to one of the obsolete claims to which family decorum or national usage have accustomed us.

What if their religious conversation is more serious? Here we must expect their religion, modest and shy as we are now presuming it to be, to disclose itself at length. Here, however, you will look in vain for the religion of Jesus.

Their standard of right and wrong is not the standard of the Gospel. They approve and condemn by a different rule. They advance principles and maintain opinions altogether opposite to the genius and character of Christianity. If we would know the truth, their opinions on the subject of religion are not formed from the perusal of the Word of God. The Bible lies on a shelf unopened. And they would be wholly ignorant of its contents, except for what they hear occasionally in church. Or perhaps they retain vague traces of the truth in their memories from the lessons of childhood.

How different, then, and indeed how contradictory are these two systems. One forms itself out of the commonly received maxims of Christendom, and the other forms itself from the study of the Holy Scriptures! It would be curious to observe (in anyone who had hitherto satisfied himself with the first system) the astonishment a person would show on his first introduction to the system based on Scripture!

4 Real Christianity

How criminal, then, must this voluntary ignorance of Christianity and the Word of God appear in the sight of God. When God of His goodness has granted us such abundant means of instruction, how great must be the guilt, and how awful must be the punishment, of voluntary ignorance!

Unreasonable to expect proficiency without effort And why are we to expect knowledge without inquiry, and success without endeavor? Bountiful as is the hand of Providence, it does not bestow its gifts to seduce us into laziness. It bestows gifts to arouse us to exertion. No one expects to attain to the heights of learning, or arts, or power, or wealth, or military glory without vigorous resolution, strenuous diligence, and steady perseverance.

Yet we expect to be Christians without labor, study, or inquiry! This is the more preposterous because Christianity, a revelation from God and not an invention of man, shows us new relations with their correspondent duties. It contains also doctrines, motives, and precepts peculiar to itself. We cannot reasonably expect to become proficient accidentally, as one might learn insensibly the maxims of worldly policy, or a scheme of mere morals.

Diligent study of Scripture The diligent perusal of the Holy Scriptures would show us our past ignorances. We would cease being deceived by superficial appearances, and confounding the Gospel of Christ with the systems of philosophers. The weighty truth forgotten today that Christianity calls on us to believe the doctrines, imbibe the principles, and practice the precepts of Christ would impress us.

Scripture everywhere represents the Gospel by figures strongly calculated to impress on our minds a sense of its value. It speaks of the Gospel as light from darkness, as release from prison, as deliverance from captivity, as life from death. The early converts universally received it with thankfulness and joy. At one time, the communication of it is promised as a reward. At another, the loss of it is threatened as a punishment. And the more general extension of the Kingdom of Christ constitutes one of the leading petitions of the short prayer taught by our blessed

Savior.

What exalted conceptions of the importance of Christianity ought to fill us when we read these descriptions. Yet in vain have we "line upon line and precept upon precept" (Isaiah 28:10). Though the Gospel had been predicted, prayed and longed for, announced, characterized and rejoiced in, we scarcely accept this heavenly treasure even when it is poured in our lap in rich abundance. We turn from it coldly, or at best possess it negligently as a thing of no estimation.

But we would be impressed with a sense of the value of Christianity by the diligent study of the Word of God, that blessed storehouse of heavenly truth and consolation. In the Word we learn what we ought to believe and what to practice. Reason dictates. Revelation commands.

"Faith comes by hearing and hearing by the Word of God" (Romans 10:17). "Search the Scriptures" (John 5:39). "Be ready to give every one a reason for the hope that is in you" (1 Peter 3:15).

Such are the declarations and injunctions of the inspired writers. The commendations of those who obey the admonition confirm these injunctions. Yet is it not undeniable that with the Bible in our houses, we are ignorant of its contents? In a great measure, the bulk of the Christian world knows so little, and mistakes so greatly, the foundational principles of the religion which it professes!

At this point I will not inquire as to why those who assent to the position that the Bible is the Word of God, and who profess to rest their hopes on the Christian basis, contentedly acquiesce in a state of such lamentable ignorance. This acquiescence, however, appears to derive much secret support from two kindred opinions. One is that *it signifies little what a man believes; look to his practice.* The other (of the same family) is that *sincerity is all in all.* Let a man's opinion and conduct be what they may, provided he be sincerely convinced that they are right. Whatever way the demands of civil society require him to be dealt with among men, in the sight of God he cannot be criminal.

Two maxims of ignorance

6   Real Christianity

1. Belief does not matter.

It would take too long to set forth the various evils inherent in these popular views. It is obvious they have limitless application. The first of these maxims proceeds from the monstrous supposition that although we are accountable creatures, we shall not be called upon to account before God for the exercise of our intellectual and emotional powers. Moreover, it proceeds on that grossly fallacious assumption that a man's opinions will not influence his practice.

We need to remind the advocates of this fallacious principle that one's judgment often receives a corrupt bias from the heart and the affections. Vice is the fruitful mother of prejudice and error.

Forgetful of these truths and confusing the most important moral distinctions, they place on the same level two groups of people. The first group is composed of those who carefully weed from their hearts every false principle and occupy themselves in a sincere and warm pursuit of truth. The second group is composed of those who yield themselves implicitly to the opinions—whatever they may be—which early prepossession may have infused. It is also composed of those who yield to whatever passion, or interest, or even acquiescing lazy spirit, may have been imposed upon their minds.

2. Sincerity is what matters.

The second of the foregoing maxims, that sincerity is all in all, proceeds on this groundless supposition: The Supreme Being has not afforded us sufficient means of discriminating truth from falsehood, or right from wrong. It implies that it does not matter how wild or extravagant a man's opinions or conduct may be. They are as much the result of impartial inquiry and honest conviction as if his sentiments and actions had been strictly conformable to the rules of reason and sobriety.

Never indeed was there a principle more general in its use, more sovereign in its potency. Instances can be found in secular history of persons committing the greatest crimes with a sincere conviction of the integrity of their conduct. Scripture offers us parallels.

It was to guard us against the error we have now been

exposing that our blessed Savior forewarned His disciples: "The time cometh, that whosoever killeth you will think that he doeth God service" (John 16:2).

We must abandon any principle like this. We must compel advocates of sincerity to restore this term to its genuine significance. They must acknowledge that it implies honesty of mind, a faithful use of the means of knowledge and improvement, a desire of being instructed, humble inquiry, impartial consideration, and unprejudiced judgment.

A right understanding of sincerity

To these values we are earnestly called, accompanied with fervent prayer for the divine blessing. "Ask and you shall receive; seek, and you shall find; knock, and it shall be opened to you" (Luke 11:9-10). "Ho, everyone that thirsts, come you to the waters" (Isaiah 55:1).

Such are the comfortable assurances and gracious encouragements held out to the truly sincere inquirer. How deep will be our guilt if we slight all these benevolent offers! "How many prophets and kings have desired to hear the things that we hear, and have not heard them!" (Luke 10:24).

Great indeed are our opportunities. Great also is our responsibility. The time of reckoning will at length arrive. And when finally summoned to the bar of God to give an account of our stewardship, what plea can we have to urge in our defense? What will be our defense if we remain willingly and obstinately ignorant of the way which leads to life? What can be our defense when we have such transcendent means of knowing this way to life, and such urgent motives to its pursuit?

II
INADEQUATE CONCEPTIONS OF
HUMAN NATURE

 ook with me now to the misunderstanding prevalent about human nature among educated people who call themselves Christians. Little attention has been given this subject, and yet it is one of greatest importance. Indeed, it lies at the very root of all true religion. And it is the basis and groundwork of Christianity.

Whatever happened to sin?

Most educated, professing Christians either overlook or deny the corruption and weakness of human nature. They acknowledge there is, and always has been, a great deal of vice and wickedness. They recognize that mankind always has been prone to sensuality and selfishness, and therefore is disobedient to the more refined and liberal principles of their nature.

These educated people can cite from all ages and cultures innumerable instances of oppression, rapacity, cruelty, fraud, envy, and malice; and they cite such occurrences in both public and private life. They acknowledge that it is in vain, too often, to inform those who thus misunderstand and to convince them about judgment. They admit that you do not thus reform the hearts of men.

Although they know their duty, they will not practice it. No, they will not, even when they are forced to acknowledge that the path of virtue is also that of real interest and solid enjoyment.

9

Although these effects of human depravity are everywhere acknowledged and deplored, we cannot expect to find them traced back to their true origin.

Sin as an accident

Instead, you will merely hear talk of frailty and infirmity, of petty transgressions, of occasional failings, and of accidental incidents. These and other qualifying terms serve only to keep the true source of evil out of view. For they do not want to shock their own understanding; rather they give consolation to the pride of human nature.

The majority of professing Christians usually speak of man as a being who is naturally pure. He is inclined to all virtue. Only occasionally something draws him out of the righteous course—almost involuntarily—or he overpowers him by the violence of temptation. Vice to them is an accidental and temporary event, rather than a constitutional and habitual disorder. They view it like a poisonous plant or weed, which lives and even thrives in the human mind, but is *not* the natural growth and production of the soil.

The biblical view of sin

Far different is the humiliating language of true Christianity. From it we learn that man is an apostate creature. He has fallen from his high, original state. He is degraded in his nature, and depraved in his faculties. He is indisposed towards the good, and disposed towards evil. Prone to vice, it is natural and easy for him to sin. Disinclined toward virtue, it is difficult and arduous to seek it.

He is tainted with sin, not slightly and superficially, but radically, and to the very core of his being. Even though it may be humiliating to acknowledge these things, still this is the biblical account of man. The truth of this forcibly comes home to us, when we contrast the remains of our primitive dignity with our present state of moral degradation.

"Into what depth thou seest,
From what height fallen."
John Milton, *Paradise Lost*, Book I

Examine, first of all, the natural powers and faculties of man: his inventions, reason, judgment, memory. View his mind of "large discourse," "looking before and after," reviewing the past, thus determining for the present, and anticipating the future. See how he discerns, collects, combines, and compares. Observe that man can apprehend and admire the beauty of moral excellence.

Consider how he exercises emotions: with fear and hope; with warmth and animation; with joy and sorrow to solace and soften; with love to attach and with patience to endure. Reflect also on the power of conscience, that faithful monitor within the human breast, to enforce the conclusions of reason, and to direct and regulate the passions of the soul.

Yet with all these advantages, we must pronounce man "majestic though in ruin." "Happy, happy world!" would be the exclamation of the inhabitant of some other planet when told that a globe like ours is peopled with such creatures as these, and abounds with situations and occasions calculated to call forth the multiplied excellencies of their nature.

But turn from man's *natural* powers to his *practices*—see how he uses and applies them. Here we have another perspective. Take in the whole overview of man's endeavors. View him in every age, and climate, and nation, in every condition and period of society. Where now do you discover the characters of his exalted nature? How his reason is clouded, his affections perverted, his conscience stupefied. How do anger, envy, hatred, and revenge spring up in his wretched bosom! How he is a slave to the meanest of his appetites. What fatal propensities does he discover to evil! What inability there is to good!

Reflect upon the state of the ancient world. Not only on the benighted part of it where all lay buried in brutish ignorance and barbarism. But think also about the seats of civilized and polished nations, and the empires of taste, learning, and philosophy. Even in those chosen regions, with whatever luster the sun of knowledge poured forth its

Man's moral advantages

Man's practice

Corruption in ancient civilizations

rays, the moral darkness was so thick, "that it might be felt." Behold their sottish idolatries, their absurd superstitions, their want of natural affections, their brutish excesses, their unfeeling oppression, their savage cruelty! Look not to the illiterate and the vulgar, but to the learned and refined. Form not your ideas from the conduct of the less restrained and the more licentious. You will turn away with disgust and shame from the allowed and familiar habits of the decent and the moral. St. Paul best states the facts, and furnishes the explanation: "Because they did not like to retain God in their knowledge, He gave them over to a reprobate mind" (Romans 1:28).

The American "noble savage"

Now consider another quarter, the native inhabitants of a new hemisphere, the American continent. There the baneful practices and contagious example of the old world had never traveled. Surely among those children of nature we may expect to find the virtuous tendencies for which we have looked in vain elsewhere. Alas, our search will still be fruitless! They are represented by the historians of America, whose accounts are more favorable than those of other great authorities. Yet they speak of the American Indians as being a compound of pride, indolence, selfishness, cunning, and cruelty.

One author speaks of them as full of revenge which nothing can satiate, of a ferocity which nothing can soften, and as strangers to the most amiable sensibilities of nature. Their horrid treatment of captives taken in war, on whose bodies they feasted, after putting them to death by the most cruel tortures, is so well-known that we may spare the disgusting recital. No commendable qualities relieve this gloomy picture, except fortitude, perseverance, and zeal for the welfare of their commitments.

Are professing Christians any better?

If the behavior of pagan peoples is indefensible, what can be said for the lives of those influenced by Christianity? True it is, Christianity has set the general tone of morals much higher than it was ever found in the pagan world. She has everywhere improved the character of man, and multiplied the comforts of society. She has benefited par-

ticularly the poor and the weak, whom from the beginning she professed to take under her special care. Yet even
in this more favored situation we shall discover too many
lamentable proofs of the depravity of man. Indeed, this
depravity becomes more apparent and less excusable. For
the advantages we enjoy only increase the obligations imposed on us.

Consider the superior excellence of our moral code; the
new principles of obedience furnished by the Gospel.
Above all, consider the awful sanction given by the teachings of Christianity about a future state of retribution.
Then we can see that our responsibility is so much greater.
Yet, in spite of all our knowledge, how little has been our
progress in virtue.

Prosperity hardens the heart. Unlimited power is ever
abused. Habits of vice grow up by themselves. Those of
virtue are slow and difficult in formation. They who draw
the first pictures of virtue, and seem most enamored by her
charms, are often the least under her influence. The
merest trifles draw them aside from that line of conduct
which they most seriously recommend to others.

There are other observations to make. How can we explain the perverse and contrary dispositions of children?
(The correction of them too often baffles the most strenuous efforts of the wise and the good.) What of the various
deceits we are likely to practice upon ourselves? By such
corruption Christianity itself has been too often disgraced. The gospel of peace has been turned into an engine of cruelty. Amidst the bitterness of persecution,
every trace has disappeared of the mild and beneficient
spirit of the religion of Jesus.

Surely to any who call themselves Christians, the following statements may be justly urged as an outstanding
instance of human depravity. We enjoy the full light of
revelation; we profess to believe "that in Him we live and
move and have our being" (Acts 17:28); we enjoy the
offer of eternal glory, preached for us by the atoning blood
of His own Son. And yet we are forgetful of His benefits.
We slight His gracious proposals, or at best receive them
with cold and unaffected hearts.

What does the most committed Christian think of human depravity?

We can test the teaching about the natural depravity of man most rigidly by asking the watchful, self-denying Christian to decide the controversy. This is not done by drawing inferences from the practice of a thoughtless, dissolute world; it is done by making an appeal to the committed believer's personal experience. Go with him into your closet. Ask him his opinion of the corruption of the heart. He will tell you that he is deeply aware of its power, having learned about its strength from self-observation and long acquaintance with the workings of his own mind. He will tell you that every day reinforces this conviction. Indeed, even hourly he sees evidence to deplore his lack of simplicity of intention, his weakness of purpose, his low views, his selfish, unworthy desires, his backwardness in duty, his dullness and coldness in performing it.

The watchful Christian finds he is continually forced to confess that he feels within himself two opposite principles, and that "he cannot do the things that he would" (Romans 7:19). In the language of the Puritan Richard Hooker, "the little fruit we have in holiness, it is, God knoweth, corrupt and unsound. We put no confidence at all in it. We challenge nothing in the world for it. We dare not call God to reckoning, as if we had Him in our debt-books. Our continual suit to Him is, and must be, to bear with our infirmities, and pardon our offenses."

Such is the moral history and conditions of man. The figures of the piece may vary. The coloring may sometimes be of a darker, sometimes of a lighter hue. But the principles of the composition and the grand outlines are everywhere the same. Wherever we direct our view, we discover the depressing proofs of our depravity. Whether we look to ancient or modern times, to barbarous or to civilized nations, to the conduct of the world around us, or to the monitor within the breast, or even to what we read, hear, act, think, or feel, the same humiliating lesson is forced upon us.

The circumstances of individuals will be found to differ. The servitude of some is more rigorous than that of others. Some, too, have for a while appeared almost to have escaped from their confinement. But none are altogether pure. All without exception, in a greater or lesser degree, bear about them the disgraceful works of their captivity.

On a full and fair investigation, such must be confessed to be the state of facts. How can sin be accounted for in man? Is there any ground of explanation other than that of some original taint, some radical principle of corruption? All other solutions are unsatisfactory. The potent cause has been assigned which can completely and sufficiently account for the evil effect.

Is sin to be explained like the law of gravity?

It appears, then, that the corruption of human nature can be proved utilizing the same mode of reasoning as that which has been used successfully in establishing the existence of the principles of gravitation and understanding its laws. The doctrine has the same solid basis on which Isaac Newton raised the superstructure of his sublime science. It is not a mere speculation; it is not an uncertain, though ingenious theory, which would be the sure result of large and actual experimentation. Instead one deduces it from incontestable facts. And it harmonizes with several parts of, and accounts for various phenomena in, the great system of the universe, a further confirmation of its truths.

Here, however, revelation begins to guide our thought, and sustains the fallible theories of our unassisted reason. The Holy Scriptures speak of us as fallen creatures. In almost every page, we shall find something that is calculated to bring down man's loftiness, and to silence his pretensions.

Is sin a relational concept of man before God?

"The imagination of man's heart is evil from his youth" (Genesis 8:21). "What is man, that he should be clean; and he which is born of a woman that he should be righteous?" (Job 15:14). "How much more abominable and filthy is man, who drinketh iniquity like water?" (Job 15:16). "The Lord looked down from heaven upon the children of men, to see if there were any that did understand and seek God. They are all gone aside; they are altogether become filthy: there is none that doeth good, no, not one" (Psalm 53:2-3).

"Who can say 'I have made my heart clean, I am pure from my sin?' " (Proverbs 20:9). For "the heart is deceitful above all, and desperately wicked, who can know it?" (Jeremiah 17:9). "Behold, I was shapen in wickedness, and in sin my mother conceived me" (Psalm 51:5). "We were by nature the children of wrath, even as others, fulfilling the desires of the flesh and of the mind" (Ephesians 2:3). "O, wretched man that I am, who shall deliver me from the body of this death!" (Romans 7:24).

Passages might be multiplied upon passages, which speak the same language. And these again might be illustrated and confirmed by various other considerations, drawn from the same sacred source. Such passages refer to the need of a thorough change of heart—a renovation of our nature—as being necessary to our becoming true Christians. Saintly men also refer their good dispositions and affections to the immediate agency of the Supreme Being.

Satan is also a reality.

But the Word of God instructs us that we have to contend not only with our own natural depravity, but with the power of darkness, the Evil Spirit, who rules in the hearts of the wicked. His domination according to Scripture is so general that he is entitled "the prince of the world" (John 14:30). There is not a stronger difference between the religious system of the Scriptures, and that of nominal Christianity, than the proof which is afforded by the subject now in question.

The existence and agency of the Evil Spirit, though so distinctly and repeatedly affirmed in Scripture, are almost universally exploded in a country which professes to admit the authority of the Bible. Other doctrines of revelation—the force and meaning of which are often to a large extent explained away—are yet conceded in general terms. But we have universally abandoned the devil as a reality. We regard him as a vanishing prejudice, and a doctrine which is a discredit for any man of understanding to believe. Like ghosts and witches, and other phantoms which haunted the night of superstition, it cannot in these enlightened times stand the test of our more critical scrutiny.

What is there in the doctrine of Satan which is in itself improbable? Or what cannot be confirmed by analogy? We see that there are wicked men who are enemies to God. And we observe their malignant behavior towards their fellow-creatures; they take pleasure and often succeed in seducing others to the commission of evil. Why then should it be deemed incredible that there may be spiritual intelligences of similar inclinations who, in like manner, are permitted to tempt men to the practice of sin?

Thus what we observe in the world around us agrees with the scriptural representations of the dreadful consequences of vice. Indeed, scriptural representations of what is commonly termed inconsideration and imprudence also agree with our observations.

If such is our sad condition, what is to be done? Is there no hope?

What is to be done?

Blessed be God! We are not shut up irrevocably in this sad condition. They who have formed a true notion of their lost and helpless state will most gladly listen to good news. And they will have a high estimation of the value of such a deliverance.

Therefore it is important not to pass hastily over those important topics of the original and superinduced corruption and weakness of man. It is a discussion painful and humiliating to the pride of human nature. The mind listens to it with difficulty, nay, with a mixture of anger and disgust. Yet it is here that our foundation must be laid. Otherwise our superstructure, whatever we may think of it, will one day prove tottering and insecure.

This therefore is not a metaphysical speculation, but a practical matter. For having no sense of the malignity of our disease, and of its dreadful issue, we do not work earnestly to obtain the remedy. It should be remembered: Diligence is not *forced on us*, but *offered to us*. God furnishes our every help; yet we are always to bear in mind that we are unable of ourselves to will or to do rightly. Scripture plainly admonishes us to "work out our salvation with fear and trembling" (Philippians 2:12), to be watchful, and to "put on the whole armour of God" (Ephesians 6:11). But it is not sufficient to *assent* to the doctrine; we must also *feel* it. To this end, let us call upon the power of habit. Let us train ourselves to refer to our natural depravity. It is the primary cause of the sad instances of vice and folly which we read about or see around us; it is the reason we feel such evil inclinations in our hearts.

Ever vigilant and distrustful of ourselves, let us look with the eye of kindness and pity on the faults of others, just as we sympathize with the sick. It should not be our reproach—and ultimately our ruin—that we have these abundant means of instructions and possess them in vain.

The objection that this is how I was created

There is one formidable objection that is often raised. For the pride of man resists being humbled. Forced to abandon the plea of innocence and unable to escape from the conclusion which we have brought him to, some bold objector will stand at bay with the following argument.

"Whatever I am," he contends, "I am what my Creator made me. I inherit a nature, which you have acknowledged is depraved and prone to evil. How then can I withstand the temptations to sin which surround me at every point? If this plea cannot establish my innocence, it must excuse or at least extenuate my guilt. I am frail and weak. A Being of infinite justice and goodness will never try me by a rule which is equitable in the case of creatures of a higher nature, but which is altogether disproportionate for me."

Since the present work is addressed to those who acknowledge the authority of the Holy Scriptures, let us read the biblical answer to such an objector. "Let no man say when he is tempted, I am tempted of God: for God cannot be tempted with evil, neither tempteth He any man" (James 1:13). "The Lord is not willing that any should perish" (2 Peter 3:9).

Likewise in other passages the idea that He should so

tempt us is repelled as injurious to His character. "Have I
any pleasure at all that the wicked should die? saith the
Lord God; and not that he should return from his ways,
and live?" (Ezekiel 18:23). "For I have no pleasure in the
death of him that dieth, saith the Lord God" (Ezekiel
18:32). Indeed, almost every page of the Word of God
contains some warning or invitation to sinners. And all
those statements, addressed to a considerate mind, must
be unquestionable proofs of our present position.

It is all the more important to expose the false optimism
concerning human nature, so that it does not take away
the moral responsibility of man. Such optimism may frequently be observed to escape our notice, lurking in secret
and diffusing a general cloud of doubt or unbelief. Or it
lowers our standards of right and wrong. Or it even whis-
pers fallacious comfort, and produces a disastrous tran-
quility.

**Beware of a shal-
low optimism
concerning
human nature.**

Although the Holy Scriptures so clearly state the natural corruption and weakness of man, they always oppose
rather than tolerate (to any degree) the view that our
natural corruption and weakness lower the demands of divine justice. Those optimistic about human nature seek
somehow to excuse our transgressions of the laws of God.
Such a notion is at war with the whole scheme of redemption by the atonement of Christ.

I turn to the Christian whose imagination may be sensitive about such suggestions. Be assured that the best practical answer to such issues is reassuring. While our natural
condition may be depraved and weak, our temptations
numerous, and our Almighty Judge infinitely holy, yet the
offers of pardon, grace, and strength to penitent sinners
are universal and unlimited.

In all this there may seem to be difficulties which we
cannot fully comprehend. Yet scarcely is there an object
around us that cannot become the subject of endless doubt
and argument. All nature calls upon us to be humble. Can
it then be surprising if we are at a loss on this question, a
question which respects not the properties of matter, or of

numbers, but the councils and ways of Him whose understanding is infinite, "whose judgments are declared to be unsearchable, and His ways past finding out"? (Romans 11:33). In this our ignorance, however, we may calmly repose ourselves on His own declaration: Though "clouds and darkness are round about Him, yet righteousness and judgment are the habitation of His throne" (Psalm 97:2).

Let it also be remembered that if some things are difficult in Christianity, those things which we are most concerned about are plain and obvious. Here, then, is true wisdom to which we can attach ourselves. Wisely we can assent to what is revealed where it is above our comprehension (we do not say contrary to our reason). We believe it on the credit of what is clearly discerned, and satisfactorily established. In truth, we are all perhaps too ready to plunge into depths which are beyond our power to fathom. "Secret things belong unto the Lord our God: but those which are revealed belong unto us and to our childen for ever, that we may do all the words of this law" (Deuteronomy 29:29).

I address these words to anyone who is seriously impressed with a sense of the critical state in which we have been placed—a short and uncertain space in which to make our peace with God; a little span of life followed by the last judgment, and an eternity of unspeakable happiness or misery. It is indeed an awful and an affecting spectacle to see men busying themselves in vain speculations. Or to see them in arrogant curiosity trifle with their dearest, their everlasting interests. Well then may we adopt the language of the poet.

> "What better can we do, than prostrate fall
> Before Him reverent; and there confess
> Humbly our faults, and pardon beg; with tears
> Watering the ground, and with our sighs the air
> Frequenting, sent from hearts contrite, in sign
> Of sorrow unfeigned, and humiliation meek?"
> Milton, *Paradise Lost*, Book 10

III
INADEQUATE CONCEPTIONS OF GOD AND OF CHRISTIAN BEHAVIOR

 ost professing Christians take for granted some of the leading doctrines of the Christian faith. The Holy Scriptures teach them and established churches hold to them. They may be summarized as follows:

- That "God so loved the world, as of his tender mercy, to give his only Son Jesus Christ for our redemption" (John 3:16).

- That our blessed Lord willingly left the glory of the Father, and was made man.

- That "he was despised and rejected of men, a man of sorrows, and acquainted with grief" (Isaiah 53:3).

- That "he was wounded for our transgressions, that he was bruised for our iniquities" (Isaiah 53:5).

- That "the Lord laid on him the iniquity of us all" (Isaiah 53:6).

- That at length, "he humbled himself even to the death of the cross . . ." to the end that all those with real repentance and true faith should come to him, might not perish, but have everlasting life (Philippians 2:8).

- That "he is now at the right hand of God, making intercession" for his people (Romans 8:34).

21

- That being reconciled to God by the death of his Son, "we may come boldly unto the throne of grace, to obtain mercy and find grace to help in time of need" (Hebrews 4:16).

- That our heavenly Father "will surely give his Holy Spirit to those that ask him" (Luke 11:13).

- That the Spirit of God must dwell in us, and that "if any man have not the Spirit of Christ, he is none of his" (Romans 8:9).

- That by this divine influence we are to be "renewed in knowledge after the image of him who created us" (Colossians 3:10), and "to be filled with the fruits of righteousness, to the praise of the glory of his grace" (Philippians 1:11).

- That "being thus made meet of the inheritance of the saints in light," we shall sleep in the Lord, and that when the last trumpet shall sound, this corruption shall put on incorruption (Colossians 1:12).

- That being at length perfected after His likeness, we shall be admitted into His heavenly kingdom.

Few churchgoers can be so inattentive as to be ignorant of these truths. What vital feelings they are calculated to promote in us, of deep self-humility and abhorrence of sin. Such emotions should also stimulate humble hope, firm faith, heavenly joy, ardent love, and active, unceasing gratitude.

A major defect is the lack of a sense of sin. But it is precisely here that one uncovers a major defect in the religious life of the bulk of professing Christians. It is a defect closely connected with that which was described in the previous chapter.

"They that be whole need not a physician, but they that are sick" (Matthew 9:12). However, had we really felt the burden of our sins, and realized with deep conviction that the weight of them must finally destroy us, our heart would have danced with joy at this invitation: "Come unto me, all you that labour and are heavy laden, and I will give you rest" (Matthew 11:28). But those with little or no sense of sin scarcely pretend to believe or experience such an offer of help. Yet without this sense of sin, and therefore of need, the logic of God's grace becomes meaningless.

Therefore let the most superficial observer compare the sentiments and views of the bulk of the Christian world with the articles of faith which still appear in their creed. An amazing discrepancy must strike him! Thus, in the minds of the crowd, religion appears to be wholly excluded from the business world and the vanities of life.

But what of those who are more serious and morally upright? What are their criteria for living? Are their hearts really filled with the things, and warmed by the love, which should make them able to inspire others? Surely their minds wander or are preoccupied with the cares and business of life. He was a masterly observer of human nature, who thus portrayed the traits of a double-minded person.

"Unstaid and fickle in all other things,
Save in the constant image of the object
That is beloved."
    William Shakespeare, *Twelfth Night,* Act 2,
    Scene IV [Speaking-Orsino, Duke of Illyria]

"But how do you know," it may be asked, "that this is how such people are preoccupied? Can you look into the hearts of men?" As it has been said "out of the abundance of the heart, the mouth speaketh" (Matthew 12:34).

People prefer generalizations about religion.

Take such people aside at an opportune time and lead the conversation to the matter of religion. The most that can be done is to get them to talk in general terms about religion. They appear lost in generalizations. There is nothing specific, nor determinate. There is nothing to suggest a mind that is used to contemplate on specific realities.

Vainly you strive to bring them around to speak on this topic. One would expect the subject of God to be uppermost in the hearts of redeemed sinners. But they elude all your endeavors. If you make mention of it yourself, they do not give it a cordial welcome; indeed they greet it with unequivocal disgust. At best, the discussion remains forced and formal.

I. INADEQUATE CONCEPTION OF CHRISTIANITY

1. Inadequate Appreciation of Christ

In discussion, people may admire the excellence of our Savior's moral conduct. We will talk of His kindness, His simplicity, the self-denial and unblemished purity of His life, even His patience and meekness in the hour of death. Often, unwilling praise may be extorted from even the most irreligious.

But never do we refer to these traits as the personal attributes of Jesus Christ. We leave those traits in the abstract as if they were those of a patron, a benefactor, or even a friend. We will speak of His love, of giving Himself for us, of dying for our sins, and Who is now exalted in heaven, at the right hand of God, making intercession for us. But who would ever think that the kindness, humanity, self-denial, and patience in suffering, which we so commend in such an abstract manner, really mean anything to us personally?

Because we have the prayer books and other sources of liturgy, we do not forget the great truths of Christ. Thanks more to the compilers of such works rather than to many of the occupants of our pulpits, these truths force themselves upon our attention whenever we attend church services.

Although entertained with the decorum that befits the day, place, and religious activity, these Christian truths are too often heard with little interest. Like the legendary tales of antiquity, which may have been important to our ancestors, we cannot be expected to take them seriously. So we hear them with apparent indifference. We repeat them by rote, assuming the language of deepest humility and warmest thankfulness, with a calm, unaltered composure.

When the service is over, we dismiss them completely from our minds, until next Sunday, when once more we renew our periodic humility and gratitude. Noticing such lukewarmness, you may pardon the writer for expressing such outright condemnation. We may allow such behavior for those who, like the Unitarians, deny or explain away the distinctive truths of the Gospel. But for those who profess a sincere belief in them, this coldness is insupportable.

If the love of Christ is so languid in the bulk of nominal Christians, then their joy and trust in Him cannot be expected to be very virile.

2. Inadequate Appreciation of the Holy Spirit

The doctrine of the sanctifying operations of the Holy Spirit appears to have met with still worse treatment. The bulk of the Christian world is too little conscious of the inability of their own unaided efforts to produce holiness of heart and life. Each day they are not accustomed to using humbly and diligently God's means for the reception and the cultivation of His help. It is no exaggeration to say that, for the most part, their notions on this subject are so confused and feeble that they can scarcely be said to believe the doctrine at all.

Many would ignore the operation of the Holy Spirit.

As to the operations of the Holy Spirit, there is no sure criterion whereby one can be sure of the reality of the Spirit's workings. Pretenders of God's extraordinary assistances have never been wanting; they abuse the credulity of the foolish and try the patience of the wise. From the canting hypocrites and wild fanatics of the last century, to their less dangerous—and chiefly less successful— descendants in our day, we hear the same things: the same unwarranted claims, the same idle tales, the same low cant.

The doctrine of the Holy Spirit, in speaking negatively of it, seems only to favor the indolence of men. Professing to furnish him with a comprehensive method of becoming wise and good, it supercedes the need for a person's own personal efforts.

And yet it is true wisdom to work diligently, to curb the disorders of the emotions, and to implant and cultivate the virtues of moral character. This is the exercise of the understanding which God requires of us, which some would rationalize as being a mere matter of bodily temperament and imaginary impulses. These are contending for that which is totally unworthy of our Divine Master. It is also that which causes sensible people to view religion with suspicion and disrepute, and to discredit the cause of Christ.

3. Inadequate Conception of Christian Behavior

Thus many have too often prostituted the sacred name of true religion. It is a sad reality that fanatics and bloody persecutors, self-interested hypocrites of all kinds, have falsely called themselves Christian. We readily admit that the false pretenses and extravagant conduct of crazy fanatics and mentally unstable enthusiasts have abused and disgraced the religious affections and the doctrine of divine assistance at all times.

Such abuse is not peculiar to religion.

The Creator intended to use the powers and property of matter for our comfort and well-being. Yet we often misdirect them so they become agents of misery and death. Likewise, the elimination of liberty has displaced patriotism. Just as we would not discard liberty because people abuse it, nor patriotism, nor courage, nor reason, speech, and memory—though all abused—no more should we eliminate true religion because self-seekers have perverted it.

True religion is particularly vulnerable to emotional abuses.

At the same time we have to acknowledge that there is no way whereby we could make certain the validity of any pretensions of anyone's religious affections. We are not always able to read the hearts of men, and to discover their real characters. So we are vulnerable to false and hypocritical pretenses.

But their falsity and hypocrisy do not prove that everything is false and hypocritical. Otherwise there would be no such thing as a wise or an honest man. Why then are we so surprised and scandalized when these impostors are detected in the Church of Christ? Christ, Himself, taught us to expect this when it is said, "Did you not sow good seed in your field? whence then has it tares?" His own answer furnishes the best solution: "An enemy has done this" (Matthew 13:27, 28).

Hypocrisy is indeed detestable, and enthusiasm sufficiently mischievous to justify our guarding against its approaches with the utmost care. Let us remember, however, that we are now and then likely to draw unfavorable conclusions from unpleasant appearances. Indeed we may draw exaggerated or confused conclusions.

The mode and language in which an uneducated person will express himself on the subject of true religion will probably be uneducated. Thus it is difficult for people of refinement not to be unreasonably shocked by such common expression. On these occasions we should at least endeavor to correct the rash judgments which we may be disposed to form. We should also learn to recognize and to prize sound and just thought, even though it is disguised in a homely or simple canopy.

It was an apostle who declared that he had come to the learned and accomplished Greeks: "not with excellency of speech, or of wisdom" (1 Corinthians 1:17). From these he had studiously abstained. Otherwise it would look like his success was due to the graces of oratory, rather than to the effectiveness of his doctrines, and to the divine power which accompanied them.

Even in our own times—when the extraordinary operations and miraculous gifts of the Holy Spirit have ceased—it is necessary for men to study, prepare, and give attention to manner as well as matter. These preparations which qualify men to become teachers of religion have not been superseded. [Here the author notes the steadfast witness of the Moravian merchants in the West Indies against the slave trade. A report to the British Privy Council on the Slave Trade records their example.]

Such Christians have excelled all mankind in solid and

unequivocal proofs of the love of Christ. In addition they have excelled all in proof of the most ardent, active, and patient zeal in His service. It is a zeal tempered with prudence, and softened with meekness. Soberly, it aims at great ends by the gradual operation of well-adjusted means, supported by a courage which no danger can intimidate, and a quiet constancy which no hardship can exhaust.

II. The Validity of the Emotions within Religion

Some might object that by insisting we make our blessed Savior the object of our emotions, we degrade our religious services. We substitute a set of mere feelings in place of the worship, by this understanding. This is an objection which deserves our most serious consideration.

If it be a just objection, then it is decisive, for our religion must be unquestionably "a reasonable service" (Romans 12:1). The objector must mean either that these emotions are unreasonable in themselves, or that they are misplaced in true religion. He can scarcely argue, however, that the emotions are in their own nature unreasonable.

We shall therefore take it that this cannot be his meaning and presume he means that the emotions are misplaced generally in religion. Or he must mean that our blessed Savior is not the proper object of them.

Notion that the emotions are out of place in religion. This notion that the emotions are out of place in true religion is commonly held, for people regard emotions as the stronghold of enthusiasm. Yet men are likely to be dupes of misapplied terms. And so we have assumed religion should rather be "rational" than be considered warm and affectionate. Do not admit this claim too hastily. For indeed we shall see that it is really, if I mistake not, a gross and harmful error.

It is surely presumptuous to propose excluding from the Christian religion such a large part of the composition of man. To exclude and condemn all the most active principles of our nature is presumption indeed.

But surely our all-wise Creator had just as valuable a purpose in giving us the elemental qualities and original passions of the mind as He did in giving us the organs of our body. One of the sad evidences of our fallen condition is that they now perpetually rebel against the powers of reason and conscience. Indeed, our passions should subject themselves to these powers.

Even if revelation were silent, natural reason might in some degree believe itself to be the effect of a religion which should come from God. Its role would be to completely repair the consequences of our superinduced depravity. The schemes of mere human wisdom have indeed confessed that this was a task beyond their strength.

Of the two most celebrated systems of philosophy, one has expressly confirmed the usurpation of the passions. The other has despaired of their regulation, seeing nothing left but their extinction. The former acted like a weak government which gives independence to a rebellious province it cannot reduce. The latter formed its boasted scheme merely upon the plan of the barbarous state for its original wild inhabitants.

Man cannot drive Christianity to such miserable expedients. She does not condescend to such devices. It is her peculiar glory and her special office to bring all the faculties of our nature into their proper place of submission and dependence. Ultimately Christianity restores the whole man, complete in all his functions, to the true ends of his being: He is devoted, entire and harmonious, to the service and glory of God.

Christianity glories in the exercise of all the affections.

"My Son, give me thine heart" (Proverbs 23:26). "Thou shalt love the Lord thy God with all thy heart" (Deuteronomy 6:5). Such are the direct and comprehensive claims which the Holy Scriptures make upon us. These claims are made upon the heart.

Indeed, we can scarcely look into any part of the sacred volume without meeting abundant proofs that it is the religion of the affections which God particularly requires. Love, zeal, gratitude, joy, hope, trust; the Word specifies each of them. It does not allow for them as weaknesses. Instead the Bible commands them as our duty, and commends them to us as our acceptable worship.

Biblical references on this theme are so numerous that there would be no end to the list of citations. The reader will observe that, as a general principle, Scripture speaks with praise of the lively exercise of the passions towards their legitimate object. On the other hand, it represents as highly criminal a cold, hard, unfeeling heart. The Bible states that lukewarmness is the object of God's disgust and aversion. Yet He favors and delights in zeal and love. He promises in Scripture to take away a heart of stone, and implant a warmer and more tender nature in its place, as the effects of His returning favor; they are the work of His renewed grace.

It is the prayer of an inspired teacher on behalf of those for whom he was most interested, "that their love," already acknowledged to be great, "might abound yet more and more" (Philippians 1:9). Scripture prescribes those modes of worship which can best excite the dormant affections and keep them in lively exercise. The express addition of music and singing increases their effects.

If we look to the most eminent of the Scripture characters, we find them warm, zealous, and affectionate. When engaged in their favorite work of celebrating the goodness of their Supreme Benefactor, their souls appear to burn within them, and their hearts kindle into rapture. The powers of language are inadequate to express their transports of delight. They call on all nature to swell the chorus, and to unite with them in hallelujahs of gratitude, joy, and praise.

The man after God's own heart abounds in these glowing expressions more than any other writer. The psalmist's writings appear to have been given us in order to set the tone, as it were, to all succeeding generations. In his commentary on the Psalms, the bishop of Norwich, Dr. George Horne, seemed to be warmed by the same heavenly flame when he said: "In the language of this divine book, the praises of the church have been offered up to the throne of grace from age to age."

When it pleased God to halt the future Apostle of the Gentiles in his wild career, and to make him a monument of transforming grace, was the force of his affections diminished? Or was it not that their direction was only changed? He brought his affections entire and unabated into the service of his blessed Master. His zeal now burned even with an increase of brightness. No intensity, no continuance of sufferings could calm its zeal nor diminish the fervors of his triumphant exultations.

Finally, Scripture does not represent the worship and service of the glorified spirits in heaven as a cold, intellectual investigation. It is the worship and service of gratitude and love. Surely, then, it should be the humble endeavor of those who are promised "to be made meet to be partakers of the inheritance of the saints in light" (Colossians 1:12) to unite their hearts in these everlasting praises here on earth.

It is also necessary to guard against the view that one can estimate the quality of the religious affections chiefly by the degree of ardors, transports, raptures, or mere animal fervors to which a person by temperament is susceptible. Daily experience convinces us that people with vivid imagination and passions may thus exercise themselves quite readily. They do so without really touching their hearts. Every tolerable actor can attest to this.

But the religious affections are not to be measured by physical fervor.

Such high degrees of passion bad men may experience. At the same time good men may lack them. We may produce such emotions or they may be genuine. But they do not form the true standard which we can use to determine the real nature or strength of the religious affections.

We learn something from the daily incidents of married and domestic life about affections. Where the heart of affection is superficial and transitory, we may find evidence of neglect and unkindness.

But the passion which alone the Scriptures dignify with the name of Love is a deep and not a superficial feeling. It is fixed and permanent, and not an occasional emotion. It proves the validity of its title by actions corresponding with its nature. "If a man love me, he will keep my sayings" (John 14:23). "This is the love of God, that we keep his commandments" (1 John 5:3). This is therefore the best standard by which to try the quality of the religious affections: Do they motivate the love which keeps His commandments?

Our Savior is the proper object of our affections.

The use of the affections in religion, then, is generally consistent with reason. It will not require many words now to prove that our blessed Savior is the proper object of them.

We know that love, gratitude, joy, hope, and trust all have their appropriate objects. It is unreasonable to exercise love in the case of an object which has no excellence or desirableness; of gratitude, where there is no obligation conferred; of joy, where there is no just cause for self-congratulation; of hope, where nothing is expected; of trust, where there is no ground of reliance.

Likewise, with our Savior, "in whom dwelleth all the fulness of the Godhead bodily" (Colossians 2:9), are we ready to love Him not and adopt the language and attitudes of the avowed enemies of Christ, enemies who say "He has no form nor comeliness; and when we shall see him, there is no beauty that we should desire him"? (Isaiah 53:2).

Is it no obligation, that He who "thought it not robbery to be equal with God" should yet for our sakes, "make Himself of no reputation, and take upon Him the form of a servant . . . and become obedient unto death, even the death of the cross"? (Philippians 2:6, 7, 8).

Is it no cause of joy that "to us is born a Savior," by whom we may be "delivered from the power of darkness" and be made "meet to be partakers of the inheritance of the saints in light"? (Colossians 1:13, 12).

Can there be a hope comparable to the "hope of our calling," which is "Christ in us, the hope of glory"? (Ephesians 4:4, Colossians 1:27).

Can there be a trust preferred to the reliance on "Jesus Christ, who is the same yesterday, today, and forever"? (Hebrews 13:8). Surely such religious affections toward our Savior are not unreasonable.

Some would make the objection that by the very nature of our being, we cannot express our emotions to an invisible Being. Our finiteness shuts us out from all those means of communication and intercourse which knit and cement the union between man and man.

Scripture could hypothetically support this argument: "He that loveth not his brother whom he hath seen, how can he love God whom he hath not seen?" (1 John 4:20). At the same time, we need only look back to the Scriptures to see how the religious affections are included and taught there as a matter of utmost and serious obligation.

We have seen that excellence is the just object of love. Good in expectancy is the object of hope. Fear lies in apprehension of evil. The misfortunes and sufferings of our fellow creatures constitute the focus of pity. One might think he observes each of these passions expressed in proportion to the magnitude and consequent claims of its corresponding object. But this is by no means the case.

Take for example the exercise of pity. We read of the slaughtered thousands with less emotion than we hear about the particulars of a shocking accident which happened in the next street. It is much the same in the case of the other emotions. Our excitement over reading a novel proves that merely fictional material can affect us greatly. We also know from experience that the greatest public misfortunes are likely to affect our feelings less than the most trivial incident which happens to ourselves.

In spite of this inconsistency between the emotions and their object, and the argument that an unseen God cannot affect human emotions, Scriptures teach that it is a major operation of the Holy Spirit to relate man's emotions appropriately toward God.

Thus mature Christians exhibit in their hearts a glowing love towards their Redeemer—not superficial and unmeaningful, but constant and rational. This love results from a strong impression of the worth of its object, heightened by an abiding sense of great, merited, and continually accumulating obligations. This love demonstrates itself in growing acts of diligent obedience or of patient suffering.

Such was the religion of the holy martyrs of the sixteenth century. Look to their writings and you will find that their thoughts and affections have been much exercised in habitual views of the blessed Jesus. Persecution, distress, degradation, and contempt assailed them in vain. All these evils served only to bring their affections into *closer* contact with their object. Their love felt no lessening in force. But that was not all. It rose to *all* the emergencies of the occasion, and burned with an increase of zeal.

III. INADEQUATE CONCEPTIONS OF THE HOLY SPIRIT'S OPERATIONS

The tendency prevalent among the bulk of nominal Christians is to form a religious system for themselves, instead of taking it from the Word of God. We see this in the neglect among them of the doctrine of the influence of the Holy Spirit.

The testimony of Scripture concerning the influence of the Holy Spirit in us

If we look into the Scriptures for information on this particular issue, we learn a very different lesson. We are taught there clearly that "of ourselves we can do nothing" (John 15:5). We are reminded "we are by nature children of wrath" (Ephesians 2:3) and under the power of the evil spirit. Our understandings are naturally dark, and our hearts averse from spiritual things.

The Bible directs us to pray for the influence of the Holy Spirit to enlighten our understanding, to dispel our prejudices, to purify our corrupt minds, and to renew us after the image of our heavenly Father. The Word of God also represents this influence as originally awakening us from sleep; as enlightening us in darkness; as "quickening us when dead" (Romans 4:17); as "delivering us from the power of darkness" (Colossians 1:13); as drawing us to God; as translating us into the kingdom of his dear Son. Further metaphorical language describes Him as "creating us in Christ Jesus" (Ephesians 2:10); as dwelling in us, and walking with us.

We are therefore to "put off the old man with his deeds," and to consider ourselves as "having put on the new man, which is renewed in knowledge after the image of him that created him" (Colossians 3:9, 10). We are to be as those who are "an habitation of God through the Spirit" (Ephesians 2:22).

So expressly, particularly, and repeatedly does the Word of God teach these lessons, that one hardly sees room for any difference of opinion among those who admit its authority. Some authorities such as Dr. Philip Doddridge [1702-1751], a well-known dissenting pastor, ascribes the whole of a Christian's repentance and faith to the divine presence. Others speak of these experiences as separate occurrences, while also attributing them to the same almighty Power.

Sometimes Scripture traces different graces of the Christian character—which show especial consideration toward our fellow creatures and no less toward the Supreme Being—to this source in particular. Sometimes it refers them all collectively to this common root, as in the phrase "the fruit of the Spirit" (Galatians 5:22).

Consistent with these representations, other parts of Scripture promise aid for the production of these effects. We read about the occasional threat to withhold the Holy Spirit or about His withdrawal, a warning of punishment for the sins of men, with the most fatal consequences of the divine displeasure.

IV. MISTAKEN CONCEPTIONS OF THE TERMS OF ACCEPTANCE WITH GOD

We could, then, in contradiction to the plainest dictates of Scripture and to the ritual of our established Church reject the scriptural authority of true Christianity. But let us not shut our eyes to perceive our real state. It is to see that we undervalue the sanctifying operations of the Holy Spirit—the first fruits of our reconciliation to

God, the purchase of our Redeemer's death, and His best gift to His true disciples. It is to see that our thoughts of the blessed Savior are confused and faint, and our affections toward Him dull and lukewarm. It is to see how disproportioned our affections are in comparison to the way others perceive their own unmerited ransom from the same ruin, and have become partakers of the same inheritance.

Examine well the foundation of biblical faith. Thus we are loudly called upon to examine well our foundations. If anything is unsound and hollow here, the superstructure cannot be safe. That is why it is important to ask the nominal Christian about the means of a sinner's acceptance by God. Is it or is it not true that, in this the greatest issue of all, people too often hold very superficial, confused, and dangerous notions?

Is there not cause to fear about their future hopes when they give little more than indistinct and nominal reference to Him who "bore our sins in His own body on the tree" (1 Peter 2:24)? Do they not thereby really rest their eternal hopes on a vague, general persuasion of the unqualified mercy of the Supreme Being?

Or still more erroneously, they rely in the main on their own negative or positive merits. They think they can look upon their lives with an impartial eye and congratulate themselves on their inoffensiveness in society. They see themselves exempt at least from any gross vice. Or they yield to the admission of sometimes being accidentally betrayed into it, but maintain they never have indulged in it habitually. Even if they have done so habitually, yet still the balance of the scales between good and evil actions remains favorable—after one makes due allowance for human frailty.

These are the considerations deemed sufficient to compose their apprehensions. These are the cordials which they find to hand themselves in the moments of serious thought, or of occasional rejection. Sometimes, perhaps, in seasons of less ordinary self-complacency, they call in also to their aid the general persuasion of the unbounded mercy and pity of God.

Yet persons of this description by no means disclaim a
Savior or relinquish their title to a share in the benefits of
His death. They close their petitions with the name of
Christ. This may be chiefly from the effect of habit, or out
of decent conformity to the established faith. They surely
do it with something of the same ambiguity of principle as
was true in the case of the dying philosopher Socrates,
who ordered the customary work of homage paid to
Aesculapius, the god of medicine. *

Others go further than this. (There are many shades of
difference between those who flatly renounce and those
who cordially embrace the doctrine of redemption by
Christ.) This group of people have a general, vague, and
poorly explained dependence on our blessed Savior. Their
hopes, when they can be distinctly made out, appear ultimately to rest in this persuasion: They are now, through
Christ, members of a new dispensation. Because of this
they believe they will be tried by a more lenient rule than
they would have been subject to otherwise.

The argument of those depending on the more lenient
rule follows. "God will not now be so extreme as to mock
what we do wrong. He will dispense with the rigorous
exactions of His law—it is too strict for such frail creatures
as we to hope we can fulfill it. Christianity has moderated
the requirements of divine justice. All we need to do now
is thankfully trust in the merits of Christ for pardoning our
sins and accepting our sincere though imperfect obedience.

"Our nature inclines toward frailties and infirmities;
our situation in life exposes us to these same infirmities.
Surely God will not severely judge these frailties. It is
practice that really determines the character. We may rest
satisfied that if, on the whole, our lives are tolerably good,
we shall escape with little or no punishment. And
through Jesus Christ our Lord we shall be finally partakers
of heavenly felicity."

---

* "Crito," said Socrates, "we owe a cock to Aesculapius; pay it therefore and do
not neglect it." This referred to the offering customarily made to the god of
medicine on recovery from an illness. Actually, Socrates was about to take the
deadly poison in his suicide.

We cannot probe into the human heart. Therefore we should always speak with caution and hesitancy when we affirm or deny the existence of internal principles from what we see. But it is not difficult for one who understands the way the mind works to come to a general conclusion about those who make the above statements. These persons rely not so much on the merits of Christ, and in the agency of divine grace, as on their own power of fulfilling the moderated requirements of divine justice. One who is discerning will discover in them a disposition to belittle the seriousness of their disease. He will find them prone to excuse in themselves what they cannot fully justify, as well as enhance the merit of what they consider are their good qualities and commendable actions.

They have little idea—so little, that one might say they have no idea at all—of the importance or difficulty of the duty Scripture calls "submitting ourselves to the righteousness of God." They do not recognize our proneness to justify ourselves in God's sight rather than to acknowledge we are guilty and helpless sinners. They have never entirely renounced their own merits, and their own strength.

Therefore those who still see merit in and of themselves fail to see the natural pride of the human heart. *All these errors naturally result from the mistaken conception entertained concerning the fundamental principles of Christianity.* They do not consider Christianity a scheme for "justifying the ungodly," by Christ dying for them, "when yet sinners."

Practical consequences of such error

The practical consequences of these errors are such as one might expect. They tend to prevent that sensitivity we ought to have of our own natural misery and helplessness. Such errors suppress the deep feeling of gratitude for the merits and intercession of Christ, to whom we are wholly indebted for our reconciliation to God.

Those who err in the above manner reap consequences in kind. They overlook that will and power from first to last, to work out our own salvation. They consider too much as a contract between two parties; in such a contract each operates independently of the other, with man doing his duty and God justifying and accepting for Christ's sake. And so they are prone to deal merely with discussions of morals. They are not likely to kindle at their Savior's name, or to teach in a detailed manner of the suffering and love of their Redeemer.

When addressing others whom they think are living in habits of sin, and under the wrath of God, they advise such people to amend their ways as a preparation for their coming to Christ. They do not exhort their counselees to throw themselves with deep prostration of soul at the foot of the cross, where they can obtain pardon and find grace in time of need.

In all this, the important point is the internal state and thinking of the mind. Let us hope that in spite of all the vagueness with which men express themselves, they will have a dependence for pardon and holiness placed where it ought to be.

If the above analysis is in any way just, it may help to explain the dullness of the affections toward the blessed Savior. It also may help us to understand the lack of importance placed upon the necessity and value of the help of the Holy Spirit which so generally prevails.

We cannot expect the affections toward our blessed Lord to flourish, because they do not receive the nurture they should have. If we would love Christ affectionately, and rejoice in Him triumphantly as the first Christians did, then we must learn like them to place our entire trust in Him. To adopt the language of the apostle, we must exclaim "God forbid that I should glory, save in the cross of our Lord Jesus Christ" (Galatians 6:14); "who of God is made unto us wisdom, and righteousness, and sanctification, and redemption" (1 Corinthians 1:30).

Doubtless there have been too many who, to their eternal ruin, have abused the doctrine of salvation by grace. But the danger of this error should not blind us to the opposite error. It is an error which we must, it seems, particularly guard against in these days.

We must not consider our dependence on our blessed Savior, the only meritorious cause of our acceptance with

God, as merely formal and nominal; we must consider it real and substantial. It must not be vague, qualified, and partial; it must be direct, whole-hearted, and entire.

"Repentance toward God and faith toward our Lord Jesus Christ" was the summary of apostolic teaching (Acts 20:21). It was not an occasional invocation of the name of Christ, or a transient recognition of His authority that filled up the measure of the phrase "believing in Jesus." This we shall find no easy task. We should do well, then, to cry out in the words of an earnest and seeking follower, "Lord help thou our unbelief " (Mark 9:24).

Each of us—for himself—needs to solemnly ask the question: Have *I* fled for refuge to the appointed hope? And are we habitually looking to it, as to the only source of consolation? "Other foundation can no man lay" (1 Corinthians 3:11). There is no other ground for dependence, no other plea for pardon; but here there is hope, even to the uttermost.

Let us labor, then, to affect our hearts with a deep conviction of our need for the Redeemer, and of the value of His offer to mediate. Let us fall down humbly before the throne of God, pleading pity and pardon in the name of the Son of His love. Let us beseech Him to give us a true spirit of repentance, and of hearty, undivided faith in the Lord Jesus.

Let us not be satisfied till the sincerity of our belief is confirmed in us by such character as is exemplified by one inspired writer, who penned, "that to as many as believe Christ is precious." Let us strive to increase daily in *love* towards our blessed Savior. Let us pray earnestly that "we may be filled with joy and peace in believing, that we may abound in hope through the power of the Holy Ghost" (Romans 15:13).

Let us painstakingly put into practice the directions already given for cherishing and cultivating the principle of the love of Christ. With this view, let us labor diligently to increase in knowledge so that our affection to the Lord who bought us may be deeply rooted and rational. This we can do by frequent meditation on the incidents of our Savior's life, and still more so by reflecting on the astonishing circumstances of His death.

Let us often call to mind the state from which He proposes to rescue us; and let us look to the glories of His heavenly kingdom. Let us have daily intercourse with Him in prayer and praise, seeking dependence and confidence in dangers, and hope and joy in our brighter hours. Let us endeavor to keep Him constantly in our minds, and to render all our thoughts of Him more distinct, lively, and intelligent.

The title of Christian is a reproach to us, if we turn ourselves away from Him after whom we are named. The name of Jesus is not to be to us like Allah of the Mohammedans; or like a talisman or an amulet, worn on the arm as an external badge and symbol of a profession, thought to preserve one from evil by some mysterious and unintelligible potency.

Instead, we should allow the name of Jesus to be engraved deeply on the heart, written there by the finger of God Himself in everlasting characters. It is our sure and undoubted title to present peace and future glory. The assurance which this title conveys of a bright turning toward heaven will lighten the burdens and alleviate the sorrows of life.

In those happier moments the title Jesus will impart to us somewhat of that fullness of joy which is at God's right hand, enabling us to join even here in the heavenly hosanna: "Worthy is the Lamb that was slain, to receive power, and riches, and wisdom, and strength, and honour, and glory, and blessing" (Revelation 5:12). "Blessing, and honour, and glory, and power, be unto him that sitteth upon the throne, and unto the Lamb for ever and ever" (Revelation 5:13).

IV

INADEQUATE CONCEPTIONS CONCERNING THE NATURE AND THE DISCIPLINE OF PRACTICAL CHRISTIANITY

People commonly believe that if a man admits to the truth of Christianity in general terms, we have no reason to be dissatisfied with him. Even though he neither knows nor concerns himself with the particulars of the faith, we do not question the validity of his claim. If he is not continually guilty of any of the gross vices against his fellow creatures, then he may take the name and privileges of a Christian. The title implies no more than a somewhat formal, general assent to Christianity and a degree of morality in practice. This is little different from that which we look for in a good deist, Moslem, or Hindu.

Indifference to true doctrine, in the bulk of the Christian world, may well raise this question: Would most so-called Christians be alarmed if it were proved to them beyond a doubt that Christianity were a mere forgery? Would this occasion any great change in their conduct or mindset? Would they make any change as a result of this discovery, except in a few of their speculative opinions?

Knowing the good effects of religion upon the masses, they might still think they should attend worship occa-

Indifference to true doctrine

sionally—for the sake of example. Would not a concern for their character, their health, their domestic and social comforts, still continue to restrain them from wicked excesses? Would they not be prompted to complete their various duties according to their social and professional position? Would they not still have access to the storehouse of counsel and instruction, the rule of their conduct, the source of their peace, hope, and consolation?

Has Christianity then any uniqueness?   It is needless to ask these questions. The lives of many known unbelievers answer them, in fact. For between these unbelievers and nominal Christians, an observer would discover little difference either in conduct or thought. Even an observer intimately acquainted with both would see little variance.

How little, then, does Christianity really deserve the title of uniqueness and superiority which has been almost universally admitted. Has it preeminence, as a particular code, over all other systems of ethics? How unmerited are the praises which have been lavished upon it by its friends, praises to which even its enemies have unwarily been forced to agree so often!

Is this then what the Son of God made Himself of no reputation for, when He condescended to become our instructor and our pattern? Is this the example He left us that we might tread in His footsteps? Was it for this that the apostles of Christ voluntarily submitted to hunger and nakedness, pain and disgrace, yes, and even death when forewarned by their Master that this would be their treatment?

It is well to remember at this point an observation we have already made: The merit of Christianity is that it has raised the general standard of morals.

What value then has Christianity in society?   But let us ask this question: Are the motives of Christianity so unnecessary to its practice, that one may be spared its principles, and still have the former—the motives—with undiminished force? If so, then its doctrines are no more than a barren and inapplicable (or at least unnecessary) theory. We can replace this theory with a simpler and less costly plan.

But can it be? Is Christianity then reduced to a mere creed? Is its practical influence restricted to a few external possibilities? Does its essence consist only of a few speculative opinions and a few useless and unprofitable beliefs? And can this be the basis of that weighty distinction clearly made by the evangelist between those who accept, and those who reject the Gospel? "He that believeth on the Son hath everlasting life; and he that believeth not the Son, shall not see life but the wrath of God abideth on him" (John 3:36).

This careless attitude leads to a situation not unlike the circumnavigators from Spain and Portugal in the sixteenth century. Setting out in opposite directions, from west and east respectively, they nevertheless confronted one another at the very time when they thought the greatest distance stood between them. So the bulk of professing, nominal Christians arrive by a different course at the very same point and occupy nearly the same ground as those they thought had an opposite viewpoint—and whose beliefs they detested. By what wicked courtesy of language is it, that the name of "Christianity" has flattered this wretched system?

I. The Discipline of Christianity as Stated in Scripture

The morality of the Gospel does not consist of so slight a fabric. Throughout its nature and scope, Christianity exhibits proof of its divine origin; and its practical precepts are no less pure than its doctrines are sublime. Can the whole of language furnish injunctions any stricter in their measure or larger in their comprehension than those with which the Word of God abound? "Whatsoever ye do in *word* or *deed*, do *all* in the name of the Lord Jesus" (Colossians 3:17). "Be *ye* holy, for God is Holy" (1 Peter 1:16). "Be ye perfect, as your Father who is in heaven is perfect" (Matthew 5:48). We are commanded to be "*perfecting* holiness" (2 Corinthians 7:1) and to "go on unto *perfection"* (Hebrews 6:1).

Such are the scriptural admonitions. Surely the readers of such admonitions are not easily satisfied in such low accomplishments. Scripture confirms us in this conclusion, as does *the force* of the expression which characterizes Christians in many different verses of Scripture. It is seen also in the radical change which occurs in every man on becoming a real Christian. "Every one who hath this hope, purifieth himself even as God is pure" (1 John 3:3). True Christians are said to be "partakers of the divine nature" (2 Peter 1:4). They are created "anew in the image of Him" (Colossians 3:10), to be "temples of the Holy Ghost" (1 Corinthians 3:16). The effects of which must appear "in *all* goodness, and righteousness, and truth" (Ephesians 5:9).

Great as was the progress which the apostle Paul had made in all virtue, he declares that he still presses forward: "forgetting the things which are behind, and reaching forth unto the things which are before" (Philippians 3:13). He prays for his beloved converts that "they may be *filled* with *all* the fulness of God" (Ephesians 3:19); that "they may be filled with the fruits of righteousness" (Philippians 1:11); and that "they might walk worthy of the Lord unto *all* pleasing, being fruitful in every good work" (Colossians 1:10). From one of the petitions our Lord taught us in prayer, we may conclude it should be a habitual sentiment of our hearts that "Thy will be done in earth as it is in heaven" (Matthew 6:10).

These few quotations from the Word of God serve clearly to show the strict standards of Christian morality.

Eternal character of true Christians

I understand the essential and practical characteristic of true Christians to be this: Relying on the promises to repentant sinners of the acceptance through the Redeemer, they have renounced and disowned all other masters, and have devoted themselves sincerely and unreservedly to God. This is the very symbol which baptism daily represents to us. It is now their determined purpose to yield themselves completely to the reasonable service of their rightful Sovereign. "They are not their own" (1 Corinthians 6:19).

For true Christians, bodily and mental faculties, their naturally acquired abilities, their substance, their authority, their time, and their influence, are not instruments of their own gratification; these belong and are consecrated to the honor of God, and are employed in His service. This is the master principle to which every other must be subordinate. Whatever may previously have been the ruling passion, whatever their leading pursuit was before, whether sensual, or intellectual, whether of science, of taste, of fancy, or of feeling—it is now of minor importance in comparison. In point of fact the passion exists only at the pleasure of its true and legitimate Master, and its owner places it entirely under His direction and control.

This is the prerogative of Christianity, "to bring into captivity every thought to the obedience of Christ (2 Corinthians 10:5). They feel its power, and are resolved "to live no longer to themselves, but to him that really died for them" (2 Corinthians 5:15). They know indeed their own infirmities. They know that the way in which they have entered is narrow and difficult. But they know the encouraging assurance that "they who wait upon the Lord shall renew their strength" (Isaiah 40:31). And the great ruling principle of their future lives is to "do all to the glory of God" (1 Corinthians 10:31). This is the seminal principle which contains within it the basic elements of all true virtue.

Glorious as is the fruit of their labors, the servants of Christ, as they continue in this life, are constantly reminded in humiliating ways of their remaining imperfections. Various passions will affect them. But an accurate description of real Christians notes that they are ones who are *gradually* changed into the image of the divine Master.

True Christians will realize their imperfections.

Neither fear of misery nor the desire for happiness motivate their efforts to excel in all holiness. They love it for its own sake. It is not self-interest that urges them to obey the will of God, and to cultivate His favor. This obedience has its foundations first in a deep and humiliating sense of God's exalted majesty and infinite power. And this sense is combined with the concept of their own smallness and their sense of duty as His creatures to submit in all things to the will of their Creator.

Admiration for the infinite perfections and love of the divine character dignify their feelings. A confiding yet humble hope in His fatherly kindness and protection is the animating force of this love. This is the Christian love of God! A love made up of admiration, preference, hope, trust, and joy, and yet chastened by reverential awe that is consciously aware of a continual gratitude.

True Christians may express their faith in different temperaments.

I need at this point to express myself with caution in case I unintentionally hurt some sensitive soul. The elementary principles which have been enumerated above may exist in various degrees and proportions. We must consider a difference in the natural disposition of a person, in the private circumstances of one's past life, and in the innumerable other details which affect the shaping of one's character. These may cause a great difference in the predominant tempers of different Christians. In one the love of God, in another the fear of God may be predominant. Trust may empower one, while gratitude does so for another.

But in greater or lesser degrees, a warm appreciation of the excellencies of God will affect all believers. Common to all is the desire to devote themselves to God, to serve Him, and to be to His glory. Common to all is the desire for holiness, for continual progress toward perfection. Common to all is the abasing consciousness of their own unworthiness and of their many besetting weaknesses, weaknesses which so often corrupt the simplicity of their intentions and frustrate their purer purposes.

But some may seek to dodge from these conclusions and to argue that it is going too far to apply them to ordinary Christians. Moreover, they argue the Mosaic law does not apply to our lives today.

This is too important an issue to pass over, so we will call in the authority of Scripture about it.

Note first that the precepts of Scripture are expressed in the most general terms. There is no hint given that any persons are at liberty to consider themselves excepted from their obligation to God.

Scripture provides no escape clauses.

Second, the precepts of the Gospel contain within them abundant proof of their *universal* application. This results from their being grounded on circumstances and relations common to *all* Christians. Christians are "not their own" because "they were bought with a price" (1 Corinthians 6:20). They are not "to live unto themselves, but unto Him that died for them" (2 Corinthians 5:15). They are commanded to do the most difficult duties "that they may be the children of their Father which is in heaven" (Matthew 5:45). "Except a man be born . . . of the Spirit (and thus become one of the sons of God), he cannot enter into the kingdom of God" (John 3:5).

Scripture is of universal application.

It is because they are sons that, in scriptural language, "God has given them the Spirit of adoption" (Romans 8:15). It is only "as many as are led by the Spirit of God," that it is declared that "they are the sons of God" (Romans 8:14). Moreover, a warning announces, "If any man have not the Spirit of Christ, he is none of his" (Romans 8:9). In short, Scripture everywhere calls Christians in general the *servants* and *children* of God. The Word requires them to serve Him with submissive obedience and that affectionate promptness which belongs to these endearing relationships.

Consider next the force of the well-known passage: "Thou shalt love the Lord thy God with *all* thy heart, and with *all* thy soul, and with *all* thy might" (Deuteronomy 6:5). Consider the gravity of this injunction, stated as it were to silence the subtle reasoning of the objector, and to make the most inconsiderate mind stop and think. This passage forces on us a conclusion strikingly confirmed by other parts of Scripture; the positive commendation of the love of God to the *whole* of the Christian church. Such a passage is 2 Corinthians 13:14. Other passages such as 1 John 3:17, Romans 16:18, together with Philippians

3:19 and 1 Corinthians 16:22, speak of the consequences where God's love is not responded to or seen.

It is a deception for one to imagine that God only condemns a total rejection of Him. God also will not accept *divided* affection. He expressly declares that a single heart and single eye are indispensable requirements of us. Scripture orders us, under the figure of amassing heavenly treasure, to make the favor and service of God our *chief* pursuits for this very reason: "Where our treasure is, there will our heart be also" (Matthew 6:21).

The seriousness of drawing the heart away from God

On the strength of this principle, similar phrases often used in Scripture suggest that the wrongness of other pursuits mainly consists in that they draw the *heart* away from God. And He is the just object of preference. Scripture therefore calls for us to prefer Him over vicious affections. (Christianity is of course hostile toward them.) But that is not all. Scripture even asserts that we prefer Him over that which it normally commands us most to exercise.

"He that loveth father and mother more than me", says our blessed Savior, "is not worthy of me" (Matthew 10:37). "He that loveth son or daughter more than me, is not worthy of me" (Matthew 10:37). The spirit of these injunctions harmonizes with many commendations in Scripture of zeal for the honor of God. There are also strong expressions of disgust and abhorrence for the lukewarm. Those that are neither cold nor hot are spoken of as being more loathsome and offensive than even open and avowed enemies.

God is a jealous God.

Another category of scriptural passages that commands the promoting of the glory of God focuses on this same point. For God will allow no competitor. Honor is due Him alone.

Scripture sees idolatry, then, as the crime against which God expresses His highest resentment and announces His severest punishment. But let us not deceive ourselves. Idolatry does not consist so much in bowing the knee to idols as it does in expressing internal homage of the heart to them. It consists in feeling toward idols any of that supreme love, or reverence, or gratitude, which God reserved for Himself as His own exclusive privilege.

On the same principle, whatever else draws off the heart from Him, monopolizes our prime attention, and holds the chief place in our respect and affections—that is as much an idol to us as is an image of wood and stone before which we should fall down and worship. The Bible commands the servant of God not to set up his idol in his *heart*. It therefore repeatedly terms sensuality and covetousness *idolatry*.

The same God who declares, "My glory will I not give to another, neither my praise to graven images" (Isaiah 42:8), also declares, "Let not the wise man glory in his wisdom, neither let the mighty man glory in his might, let not the rich man glory in his riches" (Jeremiah 9:23). "No flesh may glory in His presence" (1 Corinthians 1:29). "He that glorieth, let him glory in the Lord!" (1 Corinthians 1:31). The sudden vengeance which punished the self-glorying Herod who had consented to the praise of an admiring multitude is a dreadful comment on these injunctions. For "he gave not God the glory" (Acts 12:23).

Yet I fear that few consider these declarations today. Let the great, the wise, the learned, the successful, lay them seriously to heart. Such reflection will tend to produce a disposition opposite to the proud self-complacency that grows so readily upon the human heart. It is a disposition honoring to God, and useful to man. It is a temper composed of reverence, humility, and gratitude, which delights to praise the universal Benefactor.

The necessity of this cordial, unreserved devotedness to the glory and service of God is indispensable to the character of the true Christian. Yet people generally overlook this duty. But once it is established, it serves as a fundamental principle, both for the government of the heart and the regulation of conduct. The duty of devoted service to God will prove eminently useful for making decisions in many practical situations. No other rule would so completely and so appropriately govern one's decision-making processes in such situations.

II. NOTIONS OF PRACTICAL CHRISTIANITY GENERALLY PREVALENT

I have endeavored to establish the exactness and to determine the essential character of true practical Christianity. Let us investigate in more detail the pragmatic system of the bulk of professed Christians among us.

Consider religion as the implantation of a vigorous and active principle. When one has recognized religion's authority and supremely seated it in the heart, then from there it generally expels whatever opposes it. And from the heart religion gradually brings all the affections and desires under its complete control and regulation.

But though the heart is the special residence of true religion, one may say religion possesses in a degree the ability to be everywhere present in a person—like its divine Author. Every endeavor and pursuit must acknowledge its presence. It is like the blood circulation which animates every part of the human body, and communicates its kindly influence to the smallest and remotest tissues of the anatomy.

Assumption that religion can be a small plot fenced off in conscious life

But the notion of religion entertained by many among us seems altogether different. They begin by fencing off from the field of action a certain territory that may be fruitful, and which they may have even looked at with a longing eye. Nevertheless, they see it as forbidden ground.

Next, they assign to religion a plot of land—larger or smaller according to their views and circumstances—in which it has merely a qualified jurisdiction. This done, they presume they have a right to roam at will over the spacious remainder of territory.

In other words, religion can claim only a stated proportion of their thoughts, their time, their money, and their influence. If they may give a liberal allowance to one or more of these resources, then they assume they have satisfied religion. The rest is theirs; they do with it what they please. They have paid their tithes; they have satisfied the demand of the church. Surely they have won permission to enjoy what is left without interference!

It is scarcely possible to state too strongly the mischief which results from this fundamental error. Its consequences are obvious. For it assumes the greatest part of human actions are indifferent to religion. If men are not chargeable with actual vices, they are decent in the performance of their religious duties; and they do not stray into the forbidden ground. And if they reflect the rights of the portion of land given to religion, what more can be expected from them?

So, instead of keeping at a distance from *all sin*—which alone is the surety for our safety—they will likely not care how near they approach what they conceive to be the boundary line. Indeed, if they feel they have not actually passed it, they will think that they have done no harm. It is no trespass. Thus the free and active spirit of true religion is "cribbed and hemmed in." They have stopped religion's natural tendency to expand its territory and enlarge the circle of its influence. People think they need to prescribe it, and every attempt to extend it they resist as an encroachment.

But this is not all. For whatever they can gain from religion's territory, they add this much to the sphere of freedom, where men may roam at will, free from restraint or interference. So they will, of course, narrow and press upon the limits of religion's parcel of land, almost unconsciously so. They will also consciously and deliberately push it further and further back. If religion attempts to defend its frontier, it gradually gives way. The space occupied by it diminishes until it is scarcely discernible. They extinguish its spirit and destroy its force, reducing it to little more than the nominal possessor even of its contracted area.

This metaphorical imagery of the conditions of religion is a vivid picture of our present state. We no longer recognize the promotion of the glory of God and the possession of His favor as the objects of our highest regard and most strenuous endeavors. No longer does religion furnish us with a vigorous, habitual, and universal principle of action. Instead, we set up a system for ourselves. We become our own masters. The sense of constant homage to Him and continual service for Him is irksome and galling to us. We rejoice on seeing ourselves emancipated from it, as we would if released from a state of base and servile bondage.

Thus the very tenure and conditions of life and its possessions undergo a total change. Our faculties and powers are now our own. Whatever we have is regarded more as a property than a trust. If there is still the remembrance of some permanent claim, an occasional acknowledgement of its nominal right satisfies us. We pay our "pepper-corn rental," and take our estates to ourselves in full and free enjoyment.

That is why we attach so little sense of responsibility to the possession of status, or intellectual abilities, or wealth, or other means, or instruments of usefulness. We forget the admonitions, "Give an account of thy stewardship" (Luke 16:2), "Occupy till I come" (Luke 19:13). Or when more idealistic men than usual acknowledge that we should exercise some principle greater than that of self-gratification, we hear the appeal made only on behalf of the good of society or the welfare of our families. Even then the enforcement on ourselves of obligations resulting from these relationships comes empowered by no higher authorities than those of family comfort and of worldly interest or estimation. Besides, there are multitudes who are without families, or retiring temperaments; such principles scarcely apply to them.

Therefore we have exploded the generous and quickened spirit of Christian benevolence. In its stead we have avowedly established a system of decent selfishness. Recreation is its chief business. Watering places, field sports, card playing (never failing cards!), the theater—all contribute their aid. Amusements multiply, combined and varied, "to fill up the void of a listless and languid life."

Some are taken up with sensual pleasures.

Some take up with sensual pleasures. The chief happiness of their lives consists in one species or another of animal gratification. Remember, it is not our purpose to speak of the gross and scandalous profligates who renounce all claims to the name of Christ. But we speak of those who maintain a certain decency of character and who perhaps tolerably observe the forms of religion—these we describe as *sober sensualists*. Though less impetuous and more regulated in their lifestyle, they are not less staunch and steady in pursuit of their favorite objects than the professed devotees of licentious pleasures.

"Mortify the flesh, with its affections and lusts" is the Christian *precept*. A soft luxurious course of habitual indulgence is the *practice* of the majority of modern Christians. That constant moderation, that wholesome discipline of restraint and self-denial—which are the requisite to prevent the unnoticed inroads of the bodily appetites—seem wholly unexercised.

Christianity calls her professors to a state of diligent watchfulness and active service. We speak now of people who forget alike the duties they owe to themselves and to their fellow creatures. They often act as though their life was meant only to be a state of uniform indulgence and empty, unprofitable sloth. They make the preservation of their health and spirits sources of pleasure instead of as instruments of usefulness. And so they substitute means for ends.

Others again seem attached to "pomp and vanities of this world." Magnificent houses, lavish equipment, numerous retinues of servants, splendid entertainments, and high and fashionable connections appear to constitute, in their estimation, the supreme happiness of life. It often happens that persons to whose rank and station these indulgences most properly belong, are most indifferent to them. We see more undue concern for them in people with less wealth and rank, who strive for them. But this spirit of display and competition is a direct combat to the lowly, modest, unassuming character of the true Christian.

Others value pomp and ostentation.

As there is a sober sensuality and sober avarice, so, too, there is a sober ambition. The commercial and professional world comprise the chief sphere of its influence. The seducing considerations of diligence in our careers, of

Others are ambitious.

success in our profession, of making handsome provisions for our children, beguile our better judgments. "We rise early and take late rest and eat the bread of carefulness." In our few intervals of leisure, our exhausted spirits require refreshment. But the serious concerns of our immortal souls are matters of too grave and gloomy speculation to help us refresh. So we fly to something that may better deserve the name of relaxation, until we resume the daily labors of our employment.

Meanwhile, religion seldom comes our way, and scarcely occurs in our thoughts. When we begin to feel secret misgivings about it, company soon drowns, amusements drive away, or habitual occupations unconsciously displace or smother the rising apprehension. Professional and business people can easily quiet their consciences by pleading that the need to give attention to their business leaves them no time to think on these serious matters at the present.

Know thyself.

"Know thyself " is an injunction with which the careless and lazy cannot comply. Along with this we must obey the scriptural precept, "Keep thy heart with all diligence" (Proverbs 4:23). Generally, mankind is deplorably ignorant of its true state. Few, perhaps, have any real conception of the strength of the ties which bind them to the several objects of their devotion. Nor are they aware how little they hold in regard those concerns which matter ultimately.

Nature of disloyalty

Yet I must say it: If the affections of the soul are not supremely fixed on God; and if our dominant desire and primary goal is not to possess God's favor and to promote His glory—then we are traitors in revolt against our lawful Sovereign. All the objects of our devotion which we described above, found in the different classes of society, are simply various expressions of *disloyalty*. God insists that He set up His throne in the heart, and reign in it, without a rival. If we keep Him from His right, it will matter not by what competitor. The revolt may be more open or more secret. It may be the treason of deliberate choice or of careless levity. We may find employ in services more gross or more refined.

But whether we are the slaves of avarice, sensuality, amusements, sloth, or the devotees of ambition, taste, or fashion, we alike estrange ourselves from the dominion of our rightful Sovereign. Whether our supreme rulers are vanity and self-love, or the desire of literary fame, or of military glory—it is all idolatry. The *external* acts may be different, but in principle, the loss of affection for God is the same. Unless then we return to our allegiance to God, we must prepare to meet our punishment as rebels, on that tremendous day when all false colors shall be done away. Then "that which is often highly esteemed among men, shall appear to have been an abomination in the sight of God" (Luke 16:15).

Idleness, thoughtlessness, empty amusements, the mis-application of time or of talents, the trifling away of life in frivolous occupations or unprofitable studies—we may re-gret these in those around us. But we do so only in view of their temporal results. We do not consider them in a re-ligious connection nor lament them as endangering ever-lasting happiness. So excessive vanity and inordinate am-bition are spoken of as weaknesses rather than as sins. Even covetousness itself, though a hateful passion, we scarcely see as *irreligion.*

Consider our children. We ought to think most deeply about their happiness and that they follow right prin-ciples. But here, where we can most clearly discern our real standards, how little do we reflect to our children that they are immortal beings! Health, learning, credit, the amiable and agreeable qualities, above all money and suc-cess in life—we take these seriously. But how small a con-cern do we really show for their eternal interests!

Search then the fatal and widespread effects of this fun-damental error mentioned above, not considering reli-gion as a principle of universal application and command for all life. Robbed of its best energies, religion merely takes on the form of a compilation of restraints and pro-hibitions. Then what we cannot bend, we break, rationalizing our weaknesses and pleading the clemency of

God.
This is not the language of true Christian humiliation.
For its essence is to feel the burden of sin, and to long for release from it. In the persons we have spoken about, we have noted the unconcern with which they can amuse themselves upon the borders of sin. We have seen the easy familiarity with which they can dally with sin daily in its less offensive form. This plainly shows it is not an object of aversion to them. There is no love of holiness, no endeavor to acquire it. We see no care to prepare their souls for the reception of this divine principle of humiliation; such preparation would keep out anything that would obstruct this principle's entrance or dispute its sovereignty.

Results of externalized behavior

This condition is the lamentable consequence of regarding religion as a compilation of statutes rather than as an internal principle. It is easier to converse about external actions than about habits of mind. This attitude may even suggest to one who adopts it that it has the guise of special concern for practical religion. But we know what happens to a building if the architect decides it is a waste of materials to bother about constructing any foundation.

It is certainly true and we should never forget that all claims about internal principles of holiness are vain when conduct contradicts them. But it is no less true that the only way to effectively improve conduct is by a vigilant attention to internal principle. Our Savior gave the injunction, "Make the tree good" (Matthew 12:33) as a necessary means of obtaining good fruit. The Holy Scriptures abound in admonitions to make it our chief business to cultivate our heart with all diligence; to examine into its state with impartiality; and to watch over it with continual care. Indeed, it is the heart which constitutes the man. External actions derive their whole character and meaning from the motives and dispositions of the heart, of which they are but indications.

It may appear needless to emphasize such an obvious and established truth. We can easily lose sight of this truth in the review of our religious character, however, because we habitually preoccupy ourselves with external actions.

Bad affections, like bad weeds, sprout up and flourish all too naturally, while the graces of the Christian's spirit are like exotic plants in the soil of the human heart. They require not only light and the air of heaven to quicken their growth, but constant attention and diligent care on our part to keep them healthy and vigorous. But because of the principle we condemned above, we do not use the methods to cultivate them, such as grace, moral watchfulness, and unremitting prayers to God. So we allow these moral traits to droop, and almost die, without sufficient attention. We almost wholly neglect the culture of the mind. This opens the way for unobstructed growth of other dispositions which naturally overspread and quickly possess the mind. For the most part, they go unnoticed.

Let us cite then some examples at this point. First, it is the all-encompassing reality of the character of a true Christian that, "they are walking by faith, and not by sight" (2 Corinthians 5:7). This means not only that they so believe in the future reward and punishment that they obey though tempted to forsake their duty for present gratification. It further means that the great truths revealed in Scripture, concerning the unseen world, are uppermost in their minds and habitually in their hearts.

Marks of a true Christian

This state of mind corrects the illusions of vision; it brings into nearer focus those eternal truths which are normally either wholly overlooked or appear but faintly on the horizon. For the objects of the present life fill the human eye with a false magnification because of their immediacy.

The true Christian knows from experience, however, that the eternal probably will fade from sight and the temporal will exaggerate itself. He carefully preserves those just and enlightened views of the future given to him by divine mercy. This does not mean he retires as a recluse, for he is active in the business of life, and enjoys its comforts with moderation and thankfulness.

But our Christian will not be wholly in the world, nor give up his whole soul to worldly things. For the truth sinks into his mind that "the things which are seen are temporal, but the things which are not seen are eternal" (2 Corinthians 4:18). In the tumult and bustle of life, the still small voice sobers him with the whispered statement, "the fashion of the world passes away" (1 Corinthians 7:31).

The true disposition of spirit

This disposition alone must constitute a vast difference between the habitual temper of the real Christian and that of the mass of nominal Christians. The concerns of the present world dominate them almost entirely. They know indeed that they are mortal but they do not feel it. For the truth finds its way only into their minds, but cannot gain admission to their hearts. This understanding of the mind is altogether different from that strong practical impression of the infinite importance of eternal things.

This attitude of knowing that "the night cometh, when no man can work" (John 9:4) produces a firmness of character which hardens us against the buffetings of life. It prevents the cares and interests, the good or evil of this transitory state from deeply penetrating us. This proper impression of the relative value of temporal and eternal things maintains in the soul a dignified composure throughout all of the difficulties of life. It quickens our diligence, yet moderates our zeal. It urges us to just pursuits, yet it checks any undue care about their success. It enables us in the words of Scripture "to use this world, as not abusing it" (1 Corinthians 7:31).

Second, there is another distinction between the nominal and the real Christian. For the true Christian walks in the way of religion, not by constraint, but willingly. They are to him not only safe, but comfortable "ways of pleasantness, as well as of peace" (Proverbs 3:17). Not that he is unaware of the need of constant support in continual watchfulness. For without these, his old estimate of things will return, and the former objects of his affections will resume their influence.

So with jealous care, resolute self-denial, and earnest prayers for divine help, he guards against what might darken again his enlightened judgment, or that which

might corrupt his reformed taste. Thus he makes it his unwearied endeavor to grow in the knowledge and love of
heavenly things, and he seeks to obtain a warmer admiration and a more sincere relish of their excellence.

If we consult the sacred Scripture we will find that this
is a just representation of the judgment and disposition of
true Christians. If we also consider Sunday as a day for
rest, instituted by God, we will find the contrast between
true and nominal Christians. For the latter, it is at best a
heavy day. When compelled to devote the whole of the
day to religion, they appeal against it. How often do they
find excuses for taking journeys, writing letters, balancing
accounts.

Even business itself is a recreation compared with religion. From the drudgery of this day of sacred rest they fly
for relief to their ordinary occupations. All these expedients, which desecrate Sunday and try to change its character (it might almost be said to "mitigate its horrors"),
proves plainly that for nominal Christians, religion wears
a gloomy and forbidden aspect, not a face of consolation
and joy.

III. The Desire for Human Admiration and Applause

Another contrast between the true Christian and the
views of the prevailing opinion is the desire for the admiration and applause of men. It is perhaps the most general
passion and the most commanding authority. Like a rest-
less conqueror it seems not to spare age, nor sex, nor condition of man. It takes ten thousand shapes, the most art-
ful disguises, and winds its way in secret when it dare not
openly assert itself. It is often the master passion of the
soul.

This is the principle which parents recognize with joy
in their children. Life diligently instills and nurtures it in
advancing years. Under the names of honorable ambition
and of laudable emulation, schools and colleges stimulate

**Principle of self-
significance**

and cherish it as their professed goal. Advocates of this principle might perhaps exclaim, "The extinction of it would be like the elimination of the principle of motion in the material world. Without it all would be sluggish, cold, and comfortless. We might go further and affirm that we ought never to deviate from the powers of duty to procure the applause or avoid the shame of men. We grant that the love of praise is in some instances a ridiculous, and in others a mischievous passion. But all these are only its perversion. When turned into the right direction, and applied to its true purposes, it prompts us to every dignified and generous enterprise. It moderates and qualifies the great inequalities of the human condition."

Now let us see what are the *effects* of loving praise and distinction. Men argue, "We admit that history and a misjudging world often misapply commendations and censures. We acknowledge it would be better if men always acted from a sense of right and the love of virtue, without reference to the opinion of their fellow creatures. We even allow that this is the higher form of virtue: acting independently of consequences. But it is a degree of purity which we should not expect from the majority of people."

This motive for self-praise which is but "the infirmity of noble minds," is one of real action and approved energy, they argue further. They plead, "Do not neglect a principle so universal in its influence, so valuable in its effects, and so constant in its support to the weakness of virtue! In a selfish world the lack of praise produces the effects of disinterestedness. And when public spirit is extinguished, the country suffers from the lack of patriotism."

Now clearly this principle in question is most variable in nature. It diversifies in cultures, in modes of fashion, in habits and opinion, and in different periods of history and societies. What it tolerates in one age, it forbids in another. What one country will prescribe and applaud concerning this principle, another will condemn and scorn!

Much of this philosophers and poets of the pagan world saw and acknowledged, describing it as a changeable and inconsistent principle. They lamented the fatal effects of false glory, and the inadequacies it had in renewing the peace and happiness of mankind. They condemned the pursuit of it.

But Scripture points out to us distinctly its defective and vicious nature, and reveals to us more fully its encroaching and dangerous tendencies. Scripture teaches us how, when purified from its corrupt character, we may exercise it legitimately and direct it to its true end.

Throughout its pages, Scripture reminds us that we are originally the creatures of God's formation and continually dependent on His bounty. There, too, we learn the painful lesson of man's degradation and unworthiness. We learn that humility and contrition are the dispositions of mind best suited to our fallen condition—and most acceptable in the sight of our Creator.

Humility and contrition the essential attitudes

We learn we should repress and extinguish that spirit of arrogance and self-importance which is so natural to the heart of man. It should be our habitual care to cherish and cultivate the lowly tempers. Because of the natural advantages we have over others, and also because of all our moral superiority, we need to depend entirely on the unmerited goodness of God.

It might be said that the great aim and purpose of all revelation, and especially the design of the Gospel, is to reclaim us from our natural pride and selfishness with their fatal consequences. Its purpose, then, is to bring us to a just sense of our weakness and depravity. This results in our unfeigned humility, in which we cast ourselves down and give glory to God. "No flesh may glory in His presence. He that glorieth, let him glory in the Lord" (1 Corinthians 1:29, 31). "The lofty looks of men shall be humbled, and the haughtiness of men shall be bowed down, and the Lord alone shall be exalted" (Isaiah 2:11).

It is undeniably clear that, in the judgment of the Word of God, the love of worldly admiration and applause is basically corrupt. For it tends to exalt and aggrandize ourselves; to pride ourselves on our natural or acquired endowments; or to assume credit and merit for our own qualities. It chooses this self-esteem instead of ascribing all honor and glory where they are due. It is *false*, therefore, because it exalts that which we should demean. It is also *criminal* because it intrudes on the privilege of God.

The Scriptures further instruct us that mankind is liable to error, and therefore that the world makes mistakes with its commendations. That is not all. They also remind us that its judgment is darkened and its heart depraved: thus its applauses and contempt will, for the most part, be systematically misdirected.

Note the sharp contrast when the beneficent and disinterested spirit of Christianity aspires after more than ordinary excellence. It will not fail often to disgust and offend by stirring up secret misgivings or a painful sense of inferiority. The Word of God teaches us we can profess without offense those doctrines and precepts of Christianity concurrent with worldly principles, pursuits, and systems. Yet at times, the Christian will find himself opposing and differing with those values in the world.

For these and other reasons, the follower of Christ must agree to the occasional relinquishment of worldly favor. What is more, he should even encourage a holy jealousy and a suspicion of himself, when the world lavishly and generously bestows praise on him.

Since we should set our affections on heavenly things and converse about heavenly objects—and since we should supremely and habitually desire the love and favor of God—then it follows that the love of human applause must be unhealthy. For it tends to draw down our attention to earthly concern, and to bound our desires within the narrow limits of this world. Since it is impure—colored by the tendency to desire and love too much the good opinions and commendation of man—we should view it with suspicion.

Holy Scripture warns us, then, against the inordinate desire or earnest pursuit of worldly estimation and honor. It teaches us that God calls Christians to renounce or forego these absolutely and voluntarily. But what about the case when others do bestow these honors on us for actions intrinsically good? When this happens, and we have not solicited them, Scripture teaches we are to accept them as given by Providence for a present comfort and a reward for virtue. Moreover, God instructs us that, in our general behavior and in the little particulars of conduct, we should watch for opportunities of doing little kindnesses.

In these ways we ought to have a due respect and regard for the approval and favor of man. These, however, we should not value chiefly. They might serve to aid only our own self-gratification. Instead, they should only furnish means and instruments of influence which we may turn to good account. Or we can make them subservient to the improvement and happiness of our fellow creatures, and thus be conducive to the glory of God. At the same time we must watch our hearts with the most jealous care. Otherwise pride and self-love indifferently come in and corrupt the purity of principles that taint so readily and so easily.

In the judgment of the true Christian, credit and reputation stand on ground not very different from riches. He should not prize them too highly or desire and pursue them with too much concern. However, when the hand of Providence gives them to him, he is to accept them with thankfulness and use them with moderation. He should be able to relinquish them, if it becomes necessary, without murmur.

Reputation of limited value

The true Christian will carefully guard against the ills credit and reputation can produce and foster: intrinsic and selfish temptation, and even pride and wantonness of heart. He considers them as in themselves acceptable. But from the infirmity of his nature, he views them as highly dangerous possessions. He values them chiefly as equipping him to honor his heavenly Benefactor and lessen the miseries of mankind. He does not see them as instruments of luxury or splendor, nor as ends in themselves.

Remember—Christianity proposes not to extinguish our natural desires. It promises to bring the desires under just control and direct them to their true object. In the case of both riches and of honor, it maintains the consistency of its character. But Christianity commands us not to set our hearts on earthly treasures. It reminds us that "we have in heaven a better and more enduring substance" than this world can bestow (Hebrews 10:34).

So while Christianity represses our ambition concerning earthly credit, and moderates our attachment to it, it holds forth to us another aspiration. It bids us habitually to aspire after the splendors of that better state, where there is true glory, honor, and immortality. It therefore encourages us to have a just ambition suited to our high origin and worthy of our great ability. The little, misplaced, and perishable distinctions of this world attempt in vain to satisfy this ambition, and cannot.

Inordinate love of worldly glories

Professing Christians regard worldly credit and reputation in a light which is utterly different from that given by Scripture. Indeed the *inordinate* love of *worldly glory* implies a passion which occurs even in the dimensions of common life. It is modified and directed according to everyone's fear of action. So there is the supreme love of distinction, admiration, and praise. It is the seemingly universal acceptance of flattery.

Above all, we see it in the excessive evaluation of our worldly character. We see the way others guard it with watchfulness and jealousy—as well as with excessive care when it is in danger. When attacked, we see hot resentment; when impaired or lost, we see that bitterness of suffering. We cannot all dispute these emotions—they are too obvious. We cannot deny their existence—they are too well-known. Dishonor, disgrace, and shame present images of horror too dreadful to face. Only one thing can exclude these evils—a generous spirit.

The consequences of this are natural and obvious. Although we do not publicly declare that we follow after worldly reputation, or seek to escape from worldly disfavor, we still estimate worldly reputation as the highest essential excellence. We think of worldly shame as the greatest of all possible evils.

I have said enough to make it clear that the love of worldly reputation is a subject that is highly questionable. We should bring it under control and watch it with the most jealous care. In spite of its lofty pretensions, it can by no means justify its purpose. What real intrinsic value can the love of worldly distinction have when it wholly changes its nature and character according to public opinion? This is where Christian moralists too often exhibit little evidence of real Christianity. For they often allow for this principle in their belief structure, and even commend it with too few qualifications and too little reserve. Inconsistently they argue that to covet wealth is base and sordid. But they treat the coveting of honor as the mark of a generous and exalted nature. They are too little unaware of how worldly praise fixes the affection on earthly things—and steals the heart away from God.

A distinguishing glory of Christianity is not to rest satisfied with superficial appearances but to correct the motives and purify the heart. The true Christian obeys Scripture by nowhere keeping over himself a more resolute and jealous god than the god which desires to control the yearning for human estimation and distinction. Nowhere does he more deeply feel the insufficiency of his unassisted strength. And nowhere does he more diligently and earnestly pray for divine assistance.

A real Christian may well indeed watch and pray against the inroads of this passion, for when one transgresses its just limits, he discovers a peculiar hostility to the distinguishing graces of the Christian spirit. He watches and prays because the true Christian, in humble reliance on God's help, occupies himself more in searching out and contemplating his own weaknesses. So he endeavors to acquire and maintain a just conviction of his own great unworthiness. He continually remembers that whatever distinguishes him from others is not properly his own. Rather he is altogether indebted for it to the undeserved bounty of heaven.

So he seeks habitually to preserve a just sense of the real worth of human distinction and applause. He knows that he shall covet them less when he has learned not to overrate their value. He struggles to remember how undeservedly God often bestows them and how precariously men always possess them.

Fitting praises favor and strengthen the growth of mutual confidence and affection. But even in the case of the commendations of good men, the Christian is not beguiled into an over-evaluation of them. He dare not, lest he substitute them for the place of conscience. He guards against this by reflecting how indistinctly we can discern each other's motives, how little we can enter each other's circumstances, and how wrongly therefore others—even good men—can form judgments about us or our actions. It is also more than likely that a time will come when we will have to forfeit their esteem by adhering to the dictates of our own consciences.

The true Christian endeavors then to loosely regard the favor and applause of even good men, and much more so those of the world at large. Not that he is insensible of their worth as means and instruments of usefulness and influence. But he controls the praise of men and does not hoard it up as a miser.

Acting on these principles, the true Christian will studiously and diligently use any degree of worldly reputation he may enjoy in removing or lessening prejudices. He will use it to conciliate good will and thereby make way for the less obstructive progress of truth. Providing it entertains him with candor or even with favor, he will make it his business to step forward with benevolent and useful schemes. And where it requires united efforts to obtain and preserve it, he will seek the cooperation of men of good will.

By these and various other means he strives to render his reputation—so long as he possesses it—subservient to these great ends: advancing the cause of religion and virtue, and promoting the happiness and comfort of mankind. All the while he will not transgress the rule of the scriptural precepts in order to obtain, cultivate, or preserve this reputation. He will resolutely disclaim that dangerous, subtle reasoning of "doing evil that good may come." Ready, however, to relinquish his reputation when required to do so, he will not throw it away.

The aim of the true Christian concerning his reputation before the world is like that of the Jewish ruler, of whom it was said: "We find no fault nor occasion against this Daniel—except concerning the law of his God" (Daniel 6:5). If he gives offense, it will only be where he cannot do but otherwise. If he falls into disfavor or disgrace, it will not be chargeable to any personal offense on his part, but to the false standard of the misjudging world.

When others thus mistake his characters, or misconstrue his conducts, he will not wrap up himself in a mysterious sullenness. But he will be ready, where anyone will listen to him with patience and candor, to clear up what has been dubious. He will readily explain what has been perfectly known, and by "speaking the truth in love" will correct any erroneous impressions conceived against him.

He may sometimes feel it his duty publicly to vindicate his character for unjust reproach. But at such a time he will also guard, more than ever, and watch against pride, in order that he will not be portrayed as breaching some truth or Christian charity. He will also guard at such a time against any undue concern about his worldly reputation for its own sake. When he has done what duty requires for his vindication, he will sit down with a peaceable and quiet mind. And it will be a matter of no very deep concern to him if his endeavors should have had no visible effect.

The Christian's holy calling urges him to be victorious over the world. An indifference to his disesteem and dishonor is essentially and indispensably required for this victory. He reflects on those men who "had trial of cruel mockings" (Hebrews 11:36). He remembers the words of our blessed Savior Himself, who "was despised and rejected of men" (Isaiah 53:3).

What is he, then, that he should be exempted from the common lot, or that he should think it too much to bear the scandal of his profession? If, therefore, he is creditable and popular, he considers this as beyond what he had

The true Christian's defense of his own reputation

Victory over the world

planned. But he watches, then, with double care, lest he should grow overly fond of what he may shortly have to relinquish. He meditates on the probability of experiencing events that would necessitate him subjecting himself to disgrace and even to oblivion. So when the hour arrives, these events do not take him unawares.

He finds cultivating this desire—"honour cometh from God"—the most effective means of bringing his mind into a right spirit about the love of human praise. He rises then on the wings of contemplation, until the praises and censures of men die away from his ear, and the still small voice of conscience is no longer drowned by the din of this lower world. In this lower world the sight is likely to be occupied with earthly objects, and the hearing to be engrossed with earthly cares. But there you should come within the view of that resplendent and incorruptible crown, and your ear would be regaled with heavenly melody!

Thus at chosen times, the Christian exercises himself. When from this elevated realm he descends into the plain below, and mixes in the bustle of life, he still retains the impressions of his more retired hours. By these he realizes to himself the unseen world.

Danger in excelling

But the Christian is aware that he is particularly vulnerable when he really excels. There he is in special danger, lest his originally pure motives become unconsciously and gradually corrupted, and he become concerned in anxiety about earthly favors. This may even happen when he desires to obey the biblical injunction to "let your light so shine before men, that they may see your good works, and glorify your Father which is in heaven" (Matthew 5:16).

The Christian watches himself also on small as well as on great occasions. He is well aware that the excessive desire for human praise is a passion so subtle, that there is nothing it cannot penetrate. He finds it lurking even within his own faith, where it delights especially to dwell. Where then it appears not so large in size or in a shape that is ambiguous, we should still suspect its operation. Let not the Christian allow himself to be deceived by any external differences between himself and the world around him, relying on the sincerity of his original motive. Let him beware lest through the undiscernible encroachments of the subtle usurper he be surprised, and his religion should at length have "only a name to live," being gradually robbed of its vitalizing principle.

To those who wish to conform their lives to the Word of God, we must advise a laborious watchfulness, a jealous God, and a close and frequent scrutiny of our own hearts. This is necessary so that they do not mistake their real character. Above all, let us labor with humble prayers for the divine assistance that we might fix in ourselves a deep, habitual, and practical sense of the excellence of "that honour which cometh from God," and the comparative worthlessness of all earthly reputation and preeminence. In truth, unless the affections of the soul be thus predominantly fixed on the sight of the heavenly—in preference to that of human honor—we shall not have required of ourselves that firm strength of mind which can bear disgrace and shame without yielding to pressure. Between these two states, the disregard of fame and the bearing of disgrace, there is a broad space. He who soberly thinks he has arrived at the one, must not conclude he has arrived at the other. To the one, a little moderation and quietness of spirit may be sufficient to conduct us. But to the other we can only attain by much discipline and slow advances. When we think we have made great way, we shall find reason to confess about the other trial that we had greatly (far too greatly) overrated our progress.

Affections of the soul predominantly heavenly

When thus engaged in the pursuit of this course, we must be aware of the snares that lie in our way, and of the deceit to which we will be subjected. At that point it is good to have a full and distinct conception of the disposition of mind regarding human favor which was prescribed to us in the Scriptures. Continually examine our hearts and lives to ascertain how closely we correspond to it. This will keep us from substituting contemplation in the place of action, and from giving ourselves too much to

Beware of the snares in such a course of action.

those religious meditations we have just recommended, and in doing so neglecting the common *duties* of life. This will help us from mistaking the gratification of a lazy spirit for the Christian's disregard of fame. Let it never be forgotten that we should *deserve* estimation although we should not *possess* it.

Thus the Christian principle will operate uniformly whether approved or not. More than mortal firmness must nerve it, however, in order for it to prove genuine. Yet at the same time, it must be sweetened by love and tempered by humility.

Humility also, because it reduces us in our own esteem, will moderate our claims to worldly reputation. It will check our tendency toward showiness and display, prompting us to avoid, rather than to attract, attention. Because of it we will sit down in quiet obscurity, even though we may believe we are more entitled to credit than others. Close the entrance, however, against a proud spirit. From this spirit, under certain circumstances, we can otherwise hardly free the passion of "high disdain from sense of injured merit."

False forms of renunciation

Love and humility will concur to produce a frame of mind that balances between a zealous thirst for glory and a frigid disregard (or insolent contempt) for human glory and distinction. These latter reactions are commonly traced to a slothful, sensual, and selfish spirit. Or they may stem from the consciousness of being unequal to the task. Or they may result from the disappointment in schemes of ambition or of glory. Or they may be the reaction to a little personal experience of the world's capricious and inconsistent behavior.

Yet the reaction in these cases, however deeply felt, may be far from sincere. Sometimes the over-evaluation and inordinate desire for worldly credit, though disavowed, are abundantly evident; they are apparent from the merit now assumed by the disavower for relinquishing them. Or such reaction may be seen as the sour and surly humor which betrays a gloomy and corroded mind; it is old and fretting under the irritable sense of wanting what it most wishes to possess.

How different is the character of a true Christian. It is not a character of gross sensuality, or of lazy apathy, or of dogmatizing pride, or of disappointed ambition. It is more truly independent of worldly esteem than philosophy with all her boast. For it contrasts with Epicurean selfishness, and historical pride, and cynical brutality.

The Christian character is a spirit compounded of firmness, complacency, peace, and love. It manifests itself in acts of kindness and courtesy. It is a genuine and not a pretended kindness. It is a courtesy; it is not false and superficial, but warm and sincere. In the area of popularity, it is not intoxicated or insolent. In the area of unpopularity, it is not despondent or remorseful. It is unshaken in constancy, unwearied in benevolence, firm without roughness, and diligent without civility.

If it seems that we have dwelt disproportionately long on this theme, it is because the writer sees the dangerous qualities and un-Christian tendencies of this temptation of human praise in the ruling classes of our society. It is one of the most ordinary manifestations of pride.

IV. THE COMMON ERROR OF SUBSTITUTING PLEASANT MANNERS AND BUSINESS IN THE PLACE OF TRUE RELIGION

There is a common assumption which is highly injurious to the cause of true religion. It is the exaggerated recognition of certain amiable and useful qualities of life, and the assumption that they substitute for the supreme love and fear of God.

The following assumption is commonly made. That kindness and a sweetening of spirit (that is sympathetic, benevolent, and generous in affection), together with attention to what the world esteems are domestic and social duties, and above all a life of useful busyness—these, it is assumed, can all make up for the lack of true religion. Indeed, many will declare "the difference between these qualities and religion is verbal and illogical, rather than the real and essential. For in fact, what are they but religion and action. Is it not the great end of religion, and particularly the glory of Christianity, to illuminate the bad passions, to curb violence, to control the appetite and smooth the aspirations of man, and to make us compassionate, kind, and forgiving of one another? Is it not to make us good husbands, good fathers, and good friends? Is it not to make us useful and active citizens? If the end be effective, surely it is unnecessary refinement to dispute about the means?"

Thus some bring in a fatal distinction between morality and religion. This is a great error. For there can hardly be a stronger evidence of the cursory and superficial views with which men satisfy themselves in religious affairs than the prevalence of this view. Anyone who admits the authority of Scripture must acknowledge the falsity and persuasive reasoning of such a view.

Moreover, it is obvious that the moral worth of these sweet and benevolent tempers tends to be overrated. They readily disarm us, because of their popularity and general acceptance. But they may be no more than a mask worn in public. Follow inside the home the one who displays such traits. You may find inside that home selfishness and spite that harass his own household and subject it to his unmanly tyranny.

False benevolence

Some appeal to the moral worth of good-naturedness and the useful lives of its followers as a substitute for real Christianity. This appeal is apt to be greatly overrated.

Such benevolence does disarm our severer judgment and gain upon our affections, with its kindly, complying, and apparently disinterested nature. It prompts men to flatter instead of mortifying our pride; to sympathize either with our joys or sorrows; and to abound in obliging attentions and offices of courtesy. Its obvious tendency is to produce harmony and comfort in social and domestic life.

But there are many false pretenders of such qualities who gain credit they do not deserve. Yet they wear like a mask in public before men only the better to conceal their opposite temper. For if you could strip this man of courtesy and sweetness, and lay aside his false covering, and follow him unobserved into his family—you would find another side to him. There you would find selfishness and spiteful harassing, and vexing the wretched subjects of his unmanly tyranny. If they could talk, they would tell the world another story about him.

But benevolent qualities may be genuine. Then they may more deserve the name of amiable instinct, than of moral virtues. In any case, they imply no mental struggle, no previous discipline. Such natural benevolences are apt to evaporate in times of barren sensibilities and transitory sympathies, or in indolent wishes and unproductive declarations. They do not possess that strength and energy of character which, in the face of difficulties and dangers, produce readiness in service, vigor, and perseverance in action. Destitute of proper firmness, they often encourage that vice and folly which is their specific duty to repress. They have done well if, in spite of their self-complying nature, they do not participate in wrongdoing—or the conniving of it.

Weakness of natural benevolence

So before truth and reason, natural benevolences are bad magistrates, parents, and friends. For they are defective in those very qualities which these relationships in life require. Thus defective, they are not free from selfishness. For if we trace such deficiencies to their true source, we will find it chiefly arises from an unwillingness to submit to a painful effort. (Genuine good, however, will command sacrifice!) Or the disposition arises from the fear of losing the regard in which others hold them, and the good opinion that they want to receive.

Such weak benevolence, not rooted in the true religion, is of a sickly and short-lived nature. It lacks that hardy and vigorous temperament one needs to put up with injury, or that one needs even to survive the rude shocks to which this world forever exposes one. It is only *Christian* love which is of the character that "suffereth long and is kind," which is "not easily provoked," and that "beareth

The cycle of natural benevolence

all things and endureth all things" (1 Corinthians 13:4, 5, 7).

Review the whole of life from the spring of youth with its flush of confidence and youthful, ardent hopes, to the frustrated pursuits and disappointed hopes of advancing life. A little personal experience of the selfishness of mankind has dampened out the generous warmth and kind affections we first felt. The prompt awareness and unsuspecting simplicity of our earlier years have been reproved.

Above all, ingratitude sickens the heart and chills and thickens the very life's blood of benevolence. At length, our youthful Nero—soft and susceptible—becomes a hard and cruel tyrant.

Busy doing good

As it is with natural benevolence, so it is with so-called useful lives. Again their intrinsic worth is apt to be greatly overrated. They result from a natural busyness and activity which loves to get on and move. It loves, too, to receive credit for it.

If it is acknowledged that religion tends in general to stimulate such "usefulness," then they will tend to be "religious" also. Yet if their conduct were strictly called to account, we would judge a loss of real goodness which can only come from a higher principle. If they would have had it, then it would have been seen in them, and in the influence they might have extended to others.

Suppose, however, their standard of these amiable qualities of benevolence and usefulness were greater than what we have depicted. Could they still be a substitute for the supreme love and fear of God, and the dominant desire to promote His glory?

To allow them this plea would be like allowing men to abolish the first commandment in preference to obeying the second commandment. But true religion cannot afford to make up such a composition of duties. Likewise, by this same miserable argument, some have sought to atone for a life of injustice and plunder by the strictness of their "religious" observances. Only self-deceit and partiality keeps such from seeing their discrepancy.

At this point, one may argue that the writer is not

doing justice to his opponent's argument. For the question is not: May irreligious men of useful lives be excused for neglecting their duties toward God, in exchange for the exemplary performance of their duties toward their fellow men? Rather, the question is: If one performs his duties toward his fellows, does that not mean that duties toward God are virtually and substantially done, even if not explicitly so?

To continue the debate, the answer is clear and unequivocal in the Holy Scriptures. To love and fear God, and to worship and serve Him continually, with humble and grateful hearts, is its command. Scripture tells us habitually to regard Him as our Benefactor, Sovereign, and Father. It directs us to abound in attitudes of gratitude, loyalty, and respectful affections. How can anyone deny these positive precepts? Who then is that bold intruder into the counsels of infinite wisdom who, in obvious contempt of these specific commands, dares to plead ignorance of them? On the plea of innocence, how can he violate their plain obligations? How can he reverse the means and the ends?

A God-centered life

Such a mode of argument (to say nothing of its insolent profanity) would, once admitted, afford the means for eroding away step by step every moral obligation.

But all we need is a little common honesty to refute such an argument. For it is a body without a soul. It lacks any vital, actuating principle. Christianity is "a religion of motives." Only Christian practice can flow from Christian principle. God is to be obeyed as well as worshiped "in spirit and in truth" (John 4:23).

Some would take still another tact. The enemies of religion are sometimes apt to compare the irreligious man of a naturally sweet and amiable temper, with the religious man who has a natural roughness and severity. Or he compares the irreligious man who is naturally useful, with the religious man who is naturally lazy. From these contrasts, he draws his inferences.

A false comparison

But this mode of reasoning is also unjust. Rather should

one compare persons of similar natural qualities, and instead of citing one or two examples, look at a mass of instances. This would compel them to confess the effectiveness of true religion in heightening the benevolence and increasing the usefulness of man. For true religion implants those qualities which before had no place, and gives more power to those very characters which already exist. It renders the amiable more amiable; the useful more useful; and does so with fewer inconsistencies.

Meanwhile, let true Christians always remember that they are called upon strongly to make this argument still clearer. In this way, their position is less questionable. Scripture everywhere commands you to be tender and sympathetic, diligent and useful. It is the character of that "wisdom from above"—in which you are to be proficient—that it is "gentle and easy to be intreated, full of mercy, and good fruits" (James 3:17).

How can some deny the effectiveness of Christianity in softening the heart when they see a bigoted, furious, and cruel persecutor transformed into an almost unequalled example of candor, gentleness, tenderness, and love? See, too, the example of Christ, who "went about doing good" (Acts 10:38). Imitate such examples, and "put to silence the ignorance of foolish men" (1 Peter 2:15). So you shall obey those divine injunctions of adorning the doctrine of Christ, and of "letting your light so shine before men that they may see your good works, and glorify your Father which is in heaven" (Matthew 5:16).

The rough and austere man

If, however, you are conscious that you are naturally rough and austere; or that disappointments have soured you, or prosperity puffed you up; or from whatever cause you have bad temper, roughness of manners, or harshness of language—do not despair. Remember, Scripture promises the divine agency to "take away the heart of stone and give a heart of flesh" (Ezekiel 11:19). Pray, then, earnestly and perseveringly that the blessed aid of divine grace may operate effectively in your behalf.

Beware of giving in to the evil tempers. Beware of excusing them or allowing such to continue within you under the guise of zeal for the cause of religion and virtue. Scrutinize yourself with rigorous strictness. When there is so much room for self-deceit, call in the aid of a faithful friend and confess yourself in confidence. Consider seriously that these rough and childish tempers are a direct contrast to the "meekness and gentleness of Christ."

Christians are to "put away all bitterness and wrath, anger and clamour and evil-speaking" (Ephesians 4:31). They are to be "gentle unto all men" (2 Timothy 2:24), "forbearing, forgiving, tenderhearted." Remember the apostle's declaration, "if any man bridleth not his tongue, he only seemeth to be religious and deceiveth his own heart" (James 1:26).

It is one of the characteristics of that love (without which all claims to the name of Christian are but in vain) that "it does not behave itself unseemly" (1 Corinthians 13:5). Remember then that the honor of your profession as a Christian is at stake. So be careful not to discredit it, so that by conveying an unfavorable impression of your principles and character, you should incur the guilt of putting "an offense in your brother's way"—thereby hindering the Gospel of Christ.

Examine carefully, then, to see if the un-Christian tempers which you would eradicate are not maintained in vigor by selfishness and pride. Strive then to subdue them effectively by destroying the roots from which they feed.

From the discussion above, do not think that the amiable and useful qualities of temperament, when not prompted and governed by a principle of true religion, have been spoken of too despairingly. But "they have their reward." They have inner complacency, domestic or social comforts, and are beloved in private and respected in public. But in lacking faith, "they cannot enter into the kingdom of heaven" (Matthew 5:20).

True, practical Christianity consists in devoting the heart and life to God. It is governed supremely and habitually by a desire to know God, to be disposed to God's will, and to live in His glory. Where these essential requisites are wanting, one cannot compliment it with the name of Christianity.

Dangers beset the Christian's path. On the one hand, he justly dreads an inactive and unprofitable life. On the other, he trembles for the loss of that spiritual-mindedness which is the very essence and power of his profession.

Is he too keenly engaged in worldly business? Let him carefully examine the state of his own heart. If he finds himself pursuing wealth, or status, or reputation too much, he must realize, "No man can serve two masters" (Matthew 6:24). The world evidently possesses his heart. So it is no wonder that he finds himself dulled or, rather, dead to the impression and enjoyment of spiritual things.

Let us carefully scrutinize our whole conduct to see if we have breached or omitted a duty toward God. Particularly, we need to see if we are negligent of self-examination, of secret and public prayer, of reading the Scriptures, and of other prescribed means of grace. If we find the allotment of time which should be devoted to our spiritual development lacking, let us be open about it with ourselves and remedy the situation. Otherwise, this fatal negligence will begin to affect our hearts and our conduct. So we need to ascertain if other matters that preoccupy us are not consuming too large a share of our time. By careful management, we might still fully satisfy their legitimate claims, and then devote time to our devotional life.

But if we deliberately and honestly conclude that we ought not to give these worldly affairs less of our *time*, let us endeavor at least to give them less of our *hearts*.

Let us at least have a just sense of our great weaknesses and numerous infirmities. This is a becoming spirit in those who are commanded to "work out your own salvation with fear and trembling" (Philippians 2:12). It prompts us to constant and earnest prayer. It produces that sobriety, lowliness, and tenderness of mind, that meekness of behavior and care in conduct, which are such notable characteristics of the true Christian.

This is not a state devoid of consolation. "O tarry thou the Lord's leisure, be strong and He shall comfort thy heart" (Psalm 27:14). "They that wait upon the Lord shall renew their strength" (Isaiah 40:31). "Blessed are they that mourn, for they shall be comforted" (Matthew 5:4). These divine assurances soothe and encourage the Christian's disturbed and dejected mind, and instill unconsciously a holy composure.

V. Some Other Major Defects in the Practice of Most Nominal Christians

There appears in the minds of most nominal Christians a profoundly inadequate idea of the guilt and evil of sin. It is as if religion were supposed to be no more than an affair for the police. Offenses are seen only as injuries to society, but not as offensive toward God. Even vices are differentiated. When seen in terms of the lower ranks of society, they are viewed as offensive. The same sins in the higher ranks of society are excused, because they result from great prosperity or excessive gaiety or high spiritedness. How unjust to see social evils in the lower ranks of society, yet to accept them among the higher classes as expressive of free-thinking, gallantry, jollity, and a thousand other soft and qualifying terms!

But the Word of God estimates actions by a far less accommodating standard. There we read of no *little* sins. In the Sermon on the Mount there is no distinction made between the sins of the rich and of the poor. No references are noted of one scale of morals for the higher, and another for the lower classes of society. Idolatry, fornication, lasciviousness, drunkenness, revellings, inordinate affections—the apostle classes them all with theft and murder. He pronounces in a like manner for all these sins that "they which do such things shall not inherit the kingdom of God" (Galatians 5:21).

There are no little sins.

This perspective of nominal Christians betrays the fatal absence of the principle which is the foundation of true religion. Their slight notions of the guilt and evil of sin reveal the utter lack of all reverence for the divine Majesty. This principle is justly termed in Scripture "the beginning of wisdom." There is perhaps no more significant quality which the sacred writers so emphasized and attempted to impress upon the human heart (Job 28:28, Psalm 111:10, Proverbs 1:7-9:10).

Scriptural under-standing of sin

Scripture considers sin rebellion against the sovereignty of God. Every different act of sin equally violates His law. If persevered in, it denies His sovereignty.

To the gay and careless, this may seem very harsh. Vainly fluttering in the sunshine of worldly success, they lull themselves into a false security. "But the Lord will come as a thief in the night" (1 Thessalonians 5:2). "Seeing then that all these things shall be dissolved, what manner of persons ought we to be in all holy conversation and godliness!" (2 Peter 3:11). "The wicked shall be turned into hell, and all the people that forget God" (Psalm 9:17).

One should carefully observe that these awful declarations of future punishment of sin derive additional weight from the consideration that they are not only a judicial sentence, but arise out of the settled order of things. The kingdom of God and the kingdom of Satan are both set up in the world, and to one or the other we must belong. "The righteous have passed from death unto life" (John 5:24). "They are delivered from the power of darkness, and are translated into the kingdom of God's dear Son" (Colossians 1:13). Of unforgiven sinners the Scriptures declare on the other hand, "they are of their father the devil" (John 8:44). While on earth they are called his children, "his servants," and are said "to do his works."

Notion of being born a Christian

Such a division of those of God and of Satan flatly contradicts the general notion of so many people that if one is born in a country where Christianity is the established religion, he is born a Christian. Such a view dulls the conscience, slackens the concern to form oneself after the pattern of our Lord and Master, and forgets the provisions of God's grace. The scriptural representations of the Christian upon earth are those of "a race," "a warfare," of the need to rid oneself of every encumbrance, and of the need to put on the whole armor of God.

In the language of Scripture, Christianity is not a geographical, but a moral term. It is not native of a Christian country. It is a condition of the soul. Moreover, it is not a state into which we are naturally born. It is a state into which God must translate us.

Born again! On the one hand, it is the work of the undeserved grace of God. On the other hand, God commends us to "work out our salvation with fear and trembling" (Philippians 2:12). Scripture represents Christians who are really worth the name as being "made meet for the inheritance of the saints in light" (Colossians 1:12). Conscious, therefore, of the indispensable necessity and arduous nature of the service he engages in, the true Christian sets himself to the work with vigor and pursues it with diligence.

The Christian as a Pilgrim

The Bible vividly describes the state of such a one as that of being a Pilgrim and a Stranger. All other figures and images are given a precise meaning. Of them, none is more frequently imaged in the Scriptures than that of the journey.

The Christian is but a traveler. He prepares for all of life's difficulties. He knows he must expect them in the stormy and uncertain climate of the world. But he is traveling "to a better country" of unclouded light and serenity. If the journey is a little disagreeable, he will be less likely to loiter on the way, and he can also enjoy what is beautiful and examine what is curious. Thankfulness refreshes him.

Nor does he refuse churlishly to associate with the inhabitants of the country through which he is passing. But he also knows that to the very end of his life, his journey will be through a country beset with many enemies and snares. Temptations will throng around him and seduce him from his course. At one point he will be cheered with hope and gladdened with success. Then after another he will be disquieted with doubts and dampened by disappointments.

To nominal Christians, religion is a dull, uniform affair. They have no conception of the desires and disappointments, the hopes and the fears, the joys and the sorrows which it is calculated to bring into exercise. But to
the true Christian all is life and motion. His great work
calls forth alternately the various passions of the soul. Nor
must it be imagined that his state is one of unrelieved trial
and hardship. His very labors are "labors of love." If he has
need of patience, it is "the patience of hope." If he is
cheered, he has it in constant support and in final victory
later. Thus Scripture declares that "godliness has the
promise of the life that now is, as well as of that which is to
come" (1 Timothy 4:8).

Nominal Christians also lack that great constituent of
the true Christian character, *the love of God.* Concerning
love toward God—they lack it. So they find no pleasure in
the service and worship of God. Their devotional acts re-
semble less the freewill offerings of a grateful heart than
that constrained and reluctant tribute exacted by some
hard taskmaster from his oppressed dependent.

It is of infinite value to establish in our minds a strong
and habitual sense of the first and great commandment:
"Thou shalt love the Lord thy God with all thy heart, and
with all thy soul, and with all they might" (Deuteronomy
6:4).

This passion, operative and vigorous in its very nature,
is like a master spring. It sets in motion and maintains in
action all the complicated movements of the human soul.
It soon settles all uncertain moral questions as to what is
allowed, how strictly the law of God should be observed,
and how much fear there is in our observances. The more
generous principle of love puts an end to all such discussion. Fear will deter some from acknowledged crimes.
Self-interest will bribe others to laborious services. But it
is the peculiar glory of love that it outruns the deductions
of reasoning. It scans the refuge of sophistry.

If nominal Christians are defective in the love of God,
what of their love toward their fellow men? What are the
marks of a real spirit of philanthropy, may we ask? How

does benevolence stand the shock when it comes into encounter with our own pride, our vanity, our self-love, our self-interest, our love of care or pleasure, our ambitions, or our desire of worldly esteem? Does it make us self-denied and thus liberal in helping others? Does it make us persevere in doing good in spite of ingratitude, and only make us pity the ignorance, prejudice, or malice which misrepresents our conduct or misconstrues our motives? Does it make us refrain from what we conceive may prove the harm of another fellow creature? (These and many more hard questions really test the motives of our benevolence.)

The truth is we do not remember often enough the exalted tone of scriptural morality. So we are likely to value ourselves on the heights which we attain. And yet a better acquaintance with our standard would show us how far short we fall of that standard prescribed to us. Thus in specifying the most difficult of the duties—the forgiveness and love of enemies—our Savior points out for our imitation the example of our Supreme Benefactor. In contrast to our standards of benevolence, He adds, "Be ye therefore perfect, even as your Father who is in heaven is perfect" (Matthew 5:48).

VI. Major Defect in Neglect of the Distinctive Doctrines of Christianity

But the major and radical defect of these nominal Christians is their forgetfulness of all the distinctive doctrines of the religion which they profess. These are the corruption of human nature, the atonement of the Savior, and the sanctifying influence of the Holy Spirit. This, then, is the great distinction between the religion of Christ and that of the majority of nominal Christians.

Having thought little or nothing about God—"living without God in the world" (Ephesians 2:12)—some at length find the need of religion pressing in on them. Perhaps it is illness, the loss of a friend or some loved rela-

Some become interested in religion during a crisis.

tive, or some other stroke of adversity that quickens them to think of the precariousness of life. Then they turn to seek for some more stable foundation of happiness that the world can give them.

They look inwards perhaps and become sensible that they must have offended God. So they resolve to reform. However, while wishing to reform, they do not know either the real nature of their disease, nor its true remedy. They are aware indeed, that they must "cease to do evil, and learn to do well" (Isaiah 1:16-17). They are aware they must relinquish their habits of vice and attend more or less to the duties of religion. But they have no conception of the great malice of the disease under which they suffer, or of the perfect cure offered by the Gospel, or of the manner in which the cure can be effected.

Others do so because of guilt.

Others go further than this. The dread of the wrath of God has sunk deeply into their hearts. So for a while they strive with all their might to resist their evil propensities and to walk without stumbling in the path of duty. Again and again they resolve, and each time they break their resolutions. All their endeavors fail. They become more and more convinced of their own moral weakness and of the strength of their natural corruption. Thus groaning under the enslaving power of sin, and thus experiencing the futility of employing their utmost efforts in trying to bring about their deliverance, they are tempted to give up in despair. Meanwhile, their walk is sad and comfortless.

These are pursuing the right object, but they mistake the way in which one obtains it. For the path which they tread is not that which the Gospel has provided to conduct them in true holiness.

So they seek out religious instruction. They turn over the works of our modern theologians. The advice they get is: "Be sorry indeed for your sins and discontinue in their practice. But do not be uneasy, for Christ died for the sins of the whole world. Do your utmost, discharge your duties faithfully, and fear not, for in the end all will be well. Meanwhile, you cannot do better than to read carefully such books of practical divinity as will instruct you in the principles of a Christian life."

But the Holy Scriptures call upon them to start again and to lay afresh the whole foundation of their religious faith. They must prostrate themselves before the cross of Christ, with humble penitence and deep self-abhorrence. Solemnly they must resolve to forsake all their sins, and rely on the grace of God alone for the power to keep their resolve.

The scriptural understanding of repentance

"Believe in the Lord Jesus Christ, and thou shalt be saved" (Acts 16:31). "No man", says the Lord, "cometh unto the Father but by me" (John 14:6). "I am the true vine. As the branch cannot bear fruit of itself, except it abide in the vine, no more can ye, except ye abide in me" (John 15:1, 4). "By grace are ye saved through faith, and that not of yourselves, it is the gift of God; not of works, lest any man should boast; for we are His workmanship, created in Christ Jesus unto good works" (Ephesians 2:8-10).

This is the cardinal point on which the whole of Christianity turns. "Without holiness, no man shall see the Lord" (Hebrews 12:14). The nature of that holiness which the true Christian seeks to possess is none other than the restoration of the image of God in his soul. Obtaining it depends entirely on the operation of God's Holy Spirit. The true Christian knows therefore that this holiness does not *precede* his reconciliation with God, and then be its *cause*. But he has to *follow*, and be its *effect*. In short, it is by *faith in Christ alone*, faith marked by repentance of sin.

If then, we would be "filled with wisdom and spiritual understanding" (Colossians 1:9), and if we would "walk worthy of the Lord unto all pleasing" (Colossians 1:10), then we have to *look to Jesus*. For He is the Author and Finisher of our faith.

Traits of the Christian's learning

Looking unto Jesus has six consequences for the true Christian.

1. *Looking unto Jesus!* Here we best learn the duty and

reasonableness of an absolute and unconditional surrender of soul and body to the will and service of God. "We are not our own, for we are bought with a price" (1 Corinthians 6:19, 20).

2. *Looking unto Jesus!* Here we find displayed the guilt of sin and how hateful it must be to the holiness of God. When we see that rather than sin should go unpunished, "God spared not his own Son" (Romans 8:32) and was "pleased to bruise Him and to put Him to grief" (Isaiah 53:10) for our sakes—then we begin to learn the awfulness of sin.

3. *Looking unto Jesus!* Here we may learn best to grow in the love of God! Here the certainty of His piety and love toward repenting sinners is fully demonstrated. Here then we become animated by an abiding disposition to try to please our great Benefactor, who has already proved himself so kindly disposed toward us. Here we shall feel a deep concern, of grief mingled with shame, for having conducted ourselves so unworthily of Him. Here, too, we find the nobility to love one another and be kind to one another.

4. *Looking unto Jesus!* Here we become aware of how utterly unworthy we are of all His amazing love; and we become ashamed of our most active service. It reduces our pride and diminishes our opinions about ourselves. We become less disposed to require the respect of others and feel less resentful when slighted. When we see our Lord's humiliation, and that the "servant is not greater than his Lord" (John 15:20), we are humbled, too. If we really grow in grace, we then grow in humility.

5. *Looking unto Jesus!* Here we become aware of the shortness and uncertainty of time, and sense the vanities of life as mere trifles. We lose, therefore, our relish for frolics, the race of ambition, and the gratification of luxuriousness. Here we learn to correct the world's false

estimate of things. If we walk a rough and thorny path, it is one in which Jesus has gone before us. For we see his footprints; we cannot complain.

6. *Looking unto Jesus!* Here we follow Him as the Author and Finisher of our faith. For "He ever liveth to make intercession" for His people (Hebrews 7:25). Here we pursue our labors, and fulfill our stewardship. Here we are to conduct ourselves according to the measure given us, after the example of our blessed Master whose meat and drink it was to do the will of His heavenly Father. The realization of this view gives the Christian a relish for the worship and service of the heavenly world.

Thus we should not forget that the main distinction between real Christianity and the system of the bulk of nominal Christians chiefly consists in the differing place given to the Gospel. To the latter, the truths of the Gospel are like distant stars that twinkle with a vain and idle luster. But to the real Christian, these distinctive doctrines constitute the center in which he gravitates, like the sun of his system, and the source of his light, warmth, and life. Even the Old Testament itself, though a revelation from heaven, shines with but feeble and scanty rays. But the Gospel unveils to our eyes its blessed truths, and we are called upon to behold and to enjoy "the light of the knowledge of the glory of God in the face of Jesus Christ" (2 Corinthians 4:6).

V

THE EXCELLENCE OF
REAL CHRISTIANITY

t is now necessary to draw attention to the excellencies of true Christianity which tend to be overlooked by nominal Christians.

To begin with, there is perfect harmony between the major doctrines of the faith and their practical precepts. There is also a close connection between major doctrines and the same perfect harmony between them. It is clear that the truths of the corruption of human nature, our need of reconciliation to God by the atonement of Christ, and the restoration of our original dignity by the sanctifying influence of the Holy Spirit, are all part of one, interdependent, and mutually congruous whole.

Likewise, in the chief practical precepts of Christianity there is the same essential agreement and the same mutual dependency of one upon the other. The virtues most strongly and repeatedly urged in Scripture and in which by our progress we may advance in holiness are: the fear and love of God and of Christ; love, kindness, and meekness toward our fellow men; indifference to the possessions and events of this life compared with our concern about eternity; self-denial and humility.

I have already pointed out how essential these Christian graces are which reflect upon the character of God. They are also those we should exercise toward our fellow man and in ourselves. We find also they are what mankind most needs. Moreover, when they are acquired, they all harmonize with each other in perfect and essential union.

Take the example of lovingkindness and meekness toward others. Observe the solid foundation which self-denial, temperance, and humility lay for them. The chief causes of strife and enmity among men are pride and self-importance, and the consequent courtesies they demand from others. Other causes are the over-valuation of worldly possessions, world honor, and, in consequence, a too eager competition for them. The rough edges of one man rub against those of another. The friction thus disturbs the just arrangement and regular motions of society. But Christianity files down all these roughnesses.

The superficial cover of virtue

The religious system of nominal Christians is satisfied with a tolerable appearance of virtue. While it recommends love and charity, it tolerates pride and vanity, and it even commands the excessive valuation of character. The nominal system allows a man's whole soul to be absorbed in the pursuit of the object he is following, whether it be for personal or for professional success.

While they may, for the most part, have a soft exterior and courtly demeanor, they cannot accord well with the genuine inward principle of love. Some causes of discontent, some ground of jealousy or envy will arise; some suspicion will corrode; some disappointment will sour; some slight or slander will irritate and provoke reprisals.

The more sophisticated will learn to disguise their emotions, with an exterior of politeness and humor. But it is only the art of concealing their feelings. The pencil drawings of Hogarth, the English artist, have depicted the display of the real human emotions with brutal honesty; they show the emotions to be distorted and deformed. They describe "the Hell" which is really there.

The substance of real Christianity

But true Christianity is not satisfied with merely producing a disguise of virtue. She seeks the actual substance, which will stand the scrutinizing eyes of God "who searches the heart." So if the Christian really seeks goodness, then it must be in an atmosphere where it can breathe and truly live. That is why Christianity forbids emulating others, for this degenerates almost unknowingly into envy. Indeed, envy derives its origin chiefly from pride, and a desire for self-exaltation. How can we readily love our neighbor as ourselves, then, if we consider him also as our rival, and if we are intent solely on surpassing him in the pursuit of the competition between us?

Likewise, true Christianity teaches us not to set our hearts on earthly possessions and earthly honors. It thereby provides the climate where we can really love and sincerely forgive those who are more successful than we are, or who have thwarted us in their pursuit. "Mind not high things," says the apostle (Romans 12:16). How can we take this and other Scriptures seriously, if we are irreconcilably hostile toward anyone who may have been instrumental in our frustration?

True Christianity also teaches us not to prize human esteem at a very high rate. Thereby it provides for the practice of its command to "love from the heart" those who may justly or unjustly attack our reputation and wound our character. It commands not the show but the reality of meekness and gentleness. Thus by taking away the source of anger, and the origin of discord, it provides for the maintenance of peace and the restoration of good temper among men, when it has been broken temporarily.

It is another basic excellence of true Christianity that it **Moral values** values moral attainments far higher than intellectual accomplishments. It proposes to conduct its followers to the higher heights of virtue than of knowledge.

In contrast, most of the false systems of religion, which have prevailed in the world, have proposed to reward the intellectual labor of their devotee. By drawing aside the veil which conceals esoteric knowledge and hidden mysteries, they propose to initiate him into their sacred doctrine.

In systems which proceed on this principle, it is obvious that the bulk of mankind could never be very proficient. There was, accordingly, among the nations of antiquity, one system for the learned and another for the illiterate. An opposite mode of procedure belongs to true Christianity. Without distinction, it professes an equal regard for all human beings and its message is characterized as "glad tidings to the poor."

The preference of Christianity for moral rather than for intellectual excellence is part of true wisdom. It is possible to excel where we may really obtain excellence. For how limited is the range of the greatest intellectual abilities! How scanty are the stores of the richest forms of human knowledge! Experience daily furnishes us with examples of weakness and shortsightedness and error (even in the wisest and most learned of men!) which might serve to confound the pride of human wisdom.

Not so in morals. Made at first in the likeness of God— and still bearing about us some faint traces of our exalted origin—we are offered by our blessed Redeemer the means of purifying ourselves from our corruptions and of once more regaining the image of our heavenly Father. In love (which is the compendium of almost all other virtues), in fortitude, in justice, in humility, and in all the other graces of the Christian character, God makes us capable of attaining to heights of true sanctity. Were we faithful to the means of grace with the prompting and support of the Holy Spirit in our diligent endeavors, our labors would be crowned with success.

However, it is not the purpose of this book to attempt to trace the excellencies of Christianity, although every instance of it is a fresh proof of Christianity being a revelation from God.

It is still less the intent of the writer to attempt to vindicate the divine origin of our faith. Christians have collected a great variety of the kinds of evidence in proof of Christianity. There are the proofs from prophecy, from miracles, from the character of Christ, from that of His apostles, from the nature of the doctrines of Christianity, from the nature and excellence of its practical precepts, and from the harmony we have pointed out already between the doctrinal and practical systems of Christianity.

All these, as well as other kinds of internal evidence (from contemporary writers, or from the spread and early prevalence of Christianity), all these and other lines of argument have conviction to a greater or lesser extent. But most of all, the reader should ponder how different is the basis of Christianity from every other religious system ever proposed to the world.

VI

A BRIEF INQUIRY INTO THE PRESENT STATE OF CHRISTIANITY

Religion in decline

So far we have been concerned merely with the prevailing opinions of professing Christians. Let us now extend our inquiry to the general state of Christianity in this country.

Religion has generally tended to promote the temporal welfare of political communities. This has forcibly impressed itself upon man's mind throughout history. Many have argued the merits and demerits of this connection between religion and politics. Some of these were prone to exaggerate its merits.

If religion is to be tied to politics, then fears for the future of Christianity are increased because religion has been on the decline amongst us. It continues to decline at the present moment.

We propose to compare the state of religion in this country with the previous conditions of religious affairs. But there is a preliminary observation we need to make.

There exists—established by tacit consent—in every country a general standard or tone of morals. It varies in the same community at different periods, and differs also in the various sectors of the community. Whenever this standard falls (and also not infrequently, whenever it rises too high), offending the norm of society, it suffers accordingly in public opinion.

Thus a respect for character, which is commonly the governing principle among men, becomes to a certain degree—though no further—an incitement to morality and virtue. It would be hoped that the practice would rise above that required norm. If it does not, it follows that there will not be sufficient evidence of the existence of (much less a means of estimating) a vital principle of religion. Persons of ten thousand differing sorts of passions and opinions, when members of the same community, will regulate their conduct and adjust their behavior to the general standard expected.

Note also that the causes which tend to raise or depress the standard commonly do so slowly and almost imperceptibly.

The influence Christianity has been in raising moral standards

One will hardly contest that Christianity, whenever it has prevailed, has raised the general standard of morals to a height hitherto unknown. Some behaviors, scarcely considered as blemishes of character in the most esteemed leaders of the ancient world, are recognized today by the laws of every Christian community as deserving the severest punishments.

In other instances, virtues formerly considered rare have become common. Specifically, a merciful and courteous temper has softened the rugged manners and humanized the brutal cruelty prevalent among the most polished nations of the pagan world. One can observe also that, when once produced by Christianity, these effects are produced alike in those who deny as well as in those who accept its divine origin. So when inquiring into the real state of Christianity at any period, we must be careful not to let superficial appearances mislead us.

It may help us to learn about the advancing or declining state of Christianity in Great Britain at the present time. It may be still more helpful to discover some of the causes concerned in order to see how circumstances affect it. Experience warrants—and reason justifies and explains—that persecution generally tends to quicken the vigor and extend the prevalence of that opinion which it seeks to destroy. Persecution's "devilish engine recoils back upon itself."

Christianity especially has always thrived under persecution. For at such times it has no lukewarm professors. The Christian is then reminded that his Master's kingdom is not of this world. When all on earth looks black, he looks up to heaven for consolation. Then he sees himself as a pilgrim and a stranger. For it is then as in the hour of death that he will examine well his foundations and cleave to the fundamentals.

But when religion is in a state of quiet and prosperity, the opposite effect tends to take place. The soldiers of the church militant will then tend to forget they are at war. Their ardor slackens and their zeal languishes. John Owen has made an apt comparison: Religion in a state of prosperity is like a colony that is long settled in a strange country. It is gradually assimilated in features, demeanor, and language to the native inhabitants, until at length every vestige of its distinctiveness has died away.

The fervor of religion declines with prosperity.

If this general principle of the effects of persecution and prosperity are true, then we know what to expect of the state of Christianity in our country. For it has long been embodied in an establishment which is intimately blended with our civil institutions. People generally and justly believe it has a common interest with them all. Religion has been allowed "to exalt her mitered front in courts and parliaments."

It is an establishment whose offices are extremely numerous. Unlike the priesthood of the Jews, or the Brahmins among the Hindus (one caste in entailed succession), the Christian priesthood is supplied from every class of society and is representative of nearly every family. Unlike the Roman Catholic clergy who are debarred by celibacy to form marriage ties, or the reclusive tradition of the stricter monastic orders, Christian ministers are permitted to mix without restraint through all of society.

Assume also that Christians find no handicap in advancing in all the arts and sciences, which are the sure mark of a highly cultured society.

If such are the circumstances of Christ's partners, the lot of the general community is one of rapidly rising commercial prosperity. It is then not difficult to anticipate the likely effects this prosperous state will have on vital religion, both on the clergy and the laity.

Moreover, these efforts are further exaggerated when the country in question enjoys a free constitution of government. We have already had occasion to remark that a much looser state of morals commonly prevails among the higher ranks of society than among the middle or lower classes. But when the middle classes grow daily in wealth and substance by the success of their commercial enterprises, we can expect this loosening of morals to be extended.

The multiplication of large cities, and of luxury within them, also contributes to the decline in morals. One must even confess that the spirit of commercialism does not favor the maintenance of the religious spirit in a virile and lively state.

In times like these, the strict precepts and self-denial habits of Christianity naturally slide into disuse. Even the more serious Christians are likely to become softened and less resistant to the prevailing spirit of relaxation and indulgence. In such prosperous circumstances, men in fact are apt to think little about religion.

Christianity therefore seldom occupies the attention of the bulk of nominal Christians. Thus we may expect them to be ignorant also of its tenets. They will be acquainted merely with those doctrines and principles that the law of the land commonly holds or sanctions. But whatever is unique in real Christianity and should be habitually kept in mind, this men will consider less and less, until it is almost wholly forgotten.

Still more so, Christianity declines when those elements which are incompatible by nature, such as pride, luxury, and worldly-mindedness (the general conditions accompanying the rapid rise of wealth), are allowed to increase. This decline intensifies even more, especially among the laity, if they have been subjected to the abuses of hypocrisy or fanaticism among some of the clergy.

When some would-be reformer sees these deviations and seeks to put them right, he may succeed for a while. But in turn he may deviate in the opposite direction, and create disgust because of his violence, or vulgarity, or absurdities of behavior.

Despite all these weaknesses, the divine and original character of Christianity may still be upheld. Sometimes those who are sincere about it uphold it. Or it may be upheld because of political deference for the established faith. Perhaps most often, though, Christianity's character is upheld by those who are simply not prepared to regard it as an impostor. One sees the truth of this last point in their view of Scripture. Some bolder spirits might outrightly say the Bible is a forgery. But the majority may simply profess it is genuine, but do so inconsistently and be satisfied with remaining ignorant of its contents. Yet when you press them, they may discover themselves unable to accept the most important aspects of the truth contained within it.

When causes like these develop, then the majority of people will find little or no meaning in religion. So the time fast approaches when Christianity will be almost as disavowed in the language as it is already nonexistent in the people's conduct. Then unbelief will be rated the necessary accessory of a man of fashion, and to believe will be considered an indication of a feeble mind and a limited intelligence.

The real state of Christianity in this country is similiar to what we have conjectured above. God is forgotten. His providence is explained away. We do not see God's hand. While He multiplies his comforts to us, we are not grateful. He visits us with chastisements, but we are not contrite.

The day of the week set apart for the service of religion arrives, and we give it up, without any reluctance, to vanity and self-gratification. If we do repent with a day of national humiliation, we only use it as respite from business for festive purposes. Thus we insult the Majesty of Heaven, and deliberately excuse ourselves from the solemn services of this season of penitence and recollection.

While we advance in every brand of knowledge, yet we have become less and less acquainted with Christianity. The previous chapters have pointed out the deplorable ig-

norance of the religion many of us have who believe ourselves to be orthodox Christians. Many tend to think of it
as a mere system of ethics, and at the same time have a
most inadequate idea of the nature and severity of its practical principles.

**History of the de-
cline of Chris-
tianity**

England has brought about this decline of Christianity
to a mere system of ethics by one particular cause—its history of theology. Christianity had its best days during the
time of the great reformers. Some of them suffered martyr-
dom under Queen Mary, and their successors did so in the
time of Queen Elizabeth. Among these pillars of the Prot-
estant church, we may cite John Davenant, Bishop John
Jewel, Bishop Joseph Hall, John Reynolds, Thomas
Hooker, Lancelot Andrewes, Henry Smith, Archbishop
Robert Leighton, Archbishop James Ussher, Richard
Baxter, and many others scarcely less distinguished. Their
writings evidence the distinctive doctrines of Christianity. On the deep and solid basis of these doctrinal truths,
they laid the foundations of morals proportionately broad
and exalted. [Here Wilberforce notes his unfeigned and
high respect for Richard Baxter, whose practical works are
a treasury of Christian wisdom.]

But even before the Civil War, the great fundamental
truths held by such men began to be less prominent in the
writings of other divines. During that period, many of the
sects grievously abused the distinctive doctrines of Christianity. They made the name of Christian an open scandal. [However, Wilberforce again cites that there were
many exceptions, notably such Puritans as Owen, Howe,
and Flavel, as well as Doddridge and Witherspoon of
Princeton.]

**Fatal separation
of morals and reli-
gion**

Towards the close of the seventeenth century, the divines of the established Church began to run into a different error. They professed to make it their chief end to instill in their people the moral and practical precepts of
Christianity, which they argued had been neglected. But
they did so without maintaining sufficient theological
foundations for the sinner's acceptance before God, or

without pointing out how the practical precepts of Christianity grow out of its distinctive doctrines and are inseparably connected with them.

By this fatal error the very genius and essential nature of Christianity imperceptibly changed. So Christianity no longer retained its distinctive features nor produced that appropriate spirit which had characterized its followers. The example set has continued into this century.

For the last fifty years, the press has teemed with moral essays, many of which were published periodically. These essays saw wide circulation as they accompanied entertaining religious literature that had lost the distinctives of Christianity. In this way, the fatal habit of considering Christian morals as distinct from Christian doctrines has imperceptibly gained strength.

At length in our own days, the unique doctrines of Christianity have almost disappeared from view. Even in the majority of sermons today, one can scarcely find a trace of biblical doctrine.

Another indicator of the decline of true religion is the character of novels. They, too, reflect the very low state of religion in our country. At least in sermons, the preacher has to fit his preaching into a liturgical framework that reminds us of our faith, even if the content of the sermons is itself empty. But in novels, the writer is not so tied down. In these novels, the author places religious people and clergymen in the best possible light; they have worthy exercises of instruction, reproof, counsel, and comfort. Though painted as amiable, benevolent, and forgiving, nevertheless the distinctives of Christianity for all practical purposes might never have existed.

Indeed, many of the most eminent men of letters in modern times have been professed unbelievers. Others are lukewarm in the cause of Christ, and treat with a special goodwill, attention, and respect those who publish works opposed to Christianity, works that assail openly or undermine insidiously the very foundations of the Christian hope. [Here Wilberforce refers to David Hume as one of the most acute and forward of these professing unbelievers.]

The lesson of France, before and after the Revolution, should be studied. There, several of the same causes have been in action. They have at length produced their full effect: manners corrupted, morals depraved, pleasure-seeking predominant, and above all, religion discredited. Unbelief has grown until the public disclaimer of every religious principle has resulted. Representatives of a whole nation have witnessed publicly, without the slightest disapproval, an open, unqualified denial of the very existence of God.

There are a number of people who, though concerned about the gradual decline of religion, believe this writer tends to carry things too far. They say that the degree of religion for which he contends is inconsistent with the pursuit of ordinary business life and with the well-being of society. If his views were to prevail, people would be entirely engrossed by religion and spend all their time in prayer and preaching! William Paley in his *View of the Evidences of Christianity* argues in this manner.

The real issue is still whether our representation of what Christianity requires is consistent with the Word of God, is it not? If it is, then surely it is a small matter to sacrifice a little worldly comfort and prosperity during the short span of our existence in this life, in order to secure a crown of eternal glory and the enjoyment of those pleasures which are at God's right hand forevermore. It might be added, our blessed Savior warned us that it would often be required of us to make such a sacrifice. He exhorted us therefore to have a loose grip on all worldly possessions and enjoyments.

Even if it were true that the general prevalence of vital Christianity should somewhat interfere with the interests of national wealth and exaltation, such a general support of the faith would still be unlikely. If indeed, real Christianity should come to prevail, the world would become a better place of general peace, prosperity, and joy.

With the first proclamation of the Gospel, it is true that some of the early converts were in danger of neglecting their ordinary duties. But the apostle most pointedly guarded them against such error and repeatedly urged them to perform their particular duties with increased eagerness and fidelity. In this way, they might do credit to their Christian faith. At the same time, the apostle prescribed for them that predominant love of God and of Christ, that heavenly-mindedness, that comparative indifference to the things of this world, that earnest endeavor after growth in grace and perfection in holiness—these I have already stated to be the essential characteristics of real Christianity. Those who acknowledge the apostle's consistency in teaching, and who admit his divine authority, must admit that these precepts are not incompatible with the former.

Let it be remembered that the great characteristic mark of the true Christian is his desire to please God in all his thoughts, words, and actions. This is to take the revealed Word to be the rule of his belief and practice and so "let his light shine before men" (Matthew 5:16). It is in all things to adorn the doctrine which he professes. No calling is denounced, no pursuit is forbidden, no science or art is prohibited, no pleasure is disallowed—provided it can be reconciled with this principle.

The mark of the true Christian

Yet Christianity does not favor that vehement and inordinate ardor in the pursuit of temporal objects, which progresses toward the acquisition of immense wealth, or of widely spread renown. Real Christianity does not propose to gratify the extravagant views of those mistaken politicians whose chief concern for their country is extended dominion, the command of power, and unrivaled affluence, rather than the most solid advantages of peace, comfort, and security. These men would barter comfort for greatness. In their vain reveries they forget that the nation consists of individuals, and that the true national prosperity is no other than the multiplication of personal happiness.

In fact, instead of it being true that the prevalence of real religion would produce a stagnation of life, it is in reality true that it would infallibly produce the reverse. A man would be given a new motive to carry on his vocation with vigor, whatever his employment or pursuit. It would be a motive more sustaining and dynamic than any he had by merely humanistic perspectives. His foremost concern would not be so much to succeed as it would be to have a principled life before God. So he would not be liable to the same disappointments as men who are active in labor for worldly gain or fame. And thus he would possess the true secret of a life that was both useful and happy.

Following peace with all men and looking upon them as members of the same family, entitled to justice and brotherly kindness, he would be respected and beloved by others. He would himself be free from the annoyance of those bad passions which are activated by worldly principles and are so commonly corrosive. If such men filled any country, each thus diligently discharging the duties of his own place in society without impinging the rights of others, then all the world indeed would be active and harmonious in the human family.

Such would be the happy state of a truly Christian nation. This community, peaceful at home, would be respected and beloved abroad. General integrity in all its dealings would inspire universal confidence.

Differences between nations commonly arise from mutual injuries, and still more from mutual jealousy and distrust. Of the former, there would exist no longer any ground for complaint. The latter would find nothing to attack upon. If the violence of some neighboring state should force this peaceful community to resist an unprovoked attack (strictly defensive actions caused by those hostilities in which it would be engaged), its domestic unity would double its national power.

We must acknowledge that many of the good effects which true religion produces in political societies would be produced even by a false religion—if the false religion prescribed to good morals and upheld them effectively. But the superior excellence of Christianity is seen by acknowledging the superiority of its moral code and the powerful motives and effective means which it furnishes to enable us to practice it. Also, its doctrines help to reinforce its practices by producing an attitude which corresponds with them.

If, then, Christianity is intrinsically able to promote the preservation and health of political communities, by its very character and power, what is the grand malady of nations? The answer is short. Selfishness.

The disease of selfishness assumes different forms in the different classes of society. In the great and the wealthy, it displays itself in luxury, pomp, and parade, and in all the frivolities of a sick and depraved imagination. Such imagination seeks in vain for its own gratification and is dead to the generous and energetic pursuit of an enlarged heart. In the lower classes, where it is not immobile under the weight of despotism, it manifests itself in pride and insubordination.

Various forms of selfishness

However the external effects may vary, the internal principle is the same. It is the despotism in each one to make self the great center and end of his desires and pleasures. It is the tendency to overrate his own merits and importance, and of course to magnify his claims on others and to underrate theirs on him. It is the disposition to undervalue the advantages and to overstate the disadvantages of his condition in life. The opposite to selfishness is public spirit. This is the great principle of public life—the life's breath of the state—which keeps it active and vigorous and which carries it to true greatness and glory.

It is important to notice how much Christianity in every way is set in direct hostility to selfishness. Consequently, the public welfare must be inseparable from her prevalence. One may almost say that the main object and chief concern of real Christianity is to root out our natural selfishness and to correct the false standard it would impose upon us. Christianity seeks to bring us to a just estimate of ourselves, and of all around us. It also gives a due awareness to the various claims and obligations that result from the differing relations in which we stand.

Benevolence-enlarged, vigorous, operative benevolence is her master principle.

Christian traits
that deny selfish-
ness

These are among the Christian's daily lessons: moderation in temporal pursuits and engagements; comparative indifference to the issue of worldly projects; diligence in the discharge of personal civil duties; resignation to the will of God; and patience under all the dispensations of God's providence.

Humility is one of the essential qualities which all doctrines tend to call forth and to cultivate. Indeed, humility lays the deepest and surest grounds for benevolence.

It teaches affluence to be liberal and beneficent. It teaches authority to bear its faculties with meekness, and to consider the various cares and obligations belonging to authority as being *conditions* on which that status is conferred. Humility thus softens the glare of wealth, moderates the insolence of power, and renders the inequalities of the social orders less vexing.

It teaches the underprivileged to be diligent, humble, and patient. It reminds them that their more lowly path has been allotted to them by the hand of God. And it is their part to faithfully discharge their duties and to contentedly bear their path's inconveniences. Finally, it teaches that all human distinctions will soon be done away. And the true followers of Christ will all, as children of the same Father, be admitted alike to the possession of the same heavenly inheritance.

But the Christianity which can produce effects like these must be real, not nominal; deep, not superficial. Such, therefore, is the religion we should cultivate if we would realize these pleasing speculations and arrest the progress of political decay.

In the present circumstances of this country (again viewing it from a political point of view), unless there be restored a prevalence of Christianity in some degree, we are likely to lose all the advantages which we have benefited from with true Christianity in the past. But that is not all. We will also incur all the various evils which would result from the absence of all religion.

A weak principle of religion, while politically advantageous, can hardly sustain the condition of our society. A religion of our forefathers might be entitled to some reverence. But in our days there is not merely a blind prejudice in favor of the past; even the "proper" respect for the past has declined. And this does not have the staying power to uphold a nation. For a system, if not supported by *real* persuasion of its truth, will fall to the ground.

Weak religion is no advantage to a society.

So unless we reinforce into the minds of our society something of that original principle that animated our church system in its earlier days, it is vain for us to hope that the establishment will continue for very long. In the proportion that vital Christianity can be revived, in that same proportion the church establishment is strengthened.

How can a dry, unanimated religion, like that now professed by nominal Christians, hold its place? Much more, how can it revive the general mass of mankind?

It knows little of human nature. The kind of religion we have recommended must at least be that which is most of all suited to make an impression upon the lower classes of society. If it be thought a system of ethics may regulate the conduct of the higher classes, such a one is altogether unsuitable to the lower classes.

But blessed be God, the real religion which we recommend has proved its consistency with the original character of Christianity, namely its concern for the poor. It has proved this by changing the whole condition of the mass of society in many of the most populous districts of this and other countries.

What then should we do? Inquiry is of the first importance, and the general answer to it is not difficult. The causes and nature of the decay of religion and morals among us sufficiently indicate the course of action which is expedient for us to pursue in the highest degree. We should consider the distemper, of which we are sick

What then can be done?

as a community, as a moral rather than as a political malady. Every effort should be made to raise the depressed tone of public morals. This is a duty particularly incumbent on all who are in the higher walks of life. But every person of standing, wealth, and abilities should endeavor in like manner to exhibit a similiar example and recommend it for imitation to the circle in which he moves.

Circumstanced as we now are, it is more than ever obvious that the best man is the truest patriot.

Nor is it by their personal conduct—though this will always be vital—that men of authority and influence may promote the cause of good works. Let them, whatever their role in society, encourage virtue and discourage vice. Let them enforce the laws which, by the wisdom of our forefathers, have guarded against the grosser infractions of morals. Let them favor and take part in any plans which may be formed for the advancement of morality. Above all things, let them endeavor to instruct and to improve the next generation.

But fruitless will be all attempts to sustain, much less to revive, the fainting cause of morals, unless you can in some degree restore the prevalence of evangelical Christianity.

The duty of encouraging vital religion in the church particularly passes on to all who have the disposal of ecclesiastical appointments, and, more especially, it passes on to the officers of the church.

Some have already sounded the alarm. They have justly censured the practice of allowing Christianity to degenerate into a mere system of ethics. They recommend more attention to the distinctive doctrines of our faith.

In our schools and universities, let encouragement be given to the study of the writings of those venerable divines who flourished in the purer times of Christianity. Let even a thorough knowledge of their writings be required of candidates for ordination. Let our churches no longer witness that unseemly disharmony—which has too much prevailed—between the prayers which precede and the sermon which follows.

These are not political motives, that should prompt us

to pursue this course of action. To all who have at heart the national welfare, I solemnly submit the above suggestions. They have not been urged without misgiving, lest it should appear as though the concern of eternity were melted down into a mere matter of temporal advantage, or of political expediency.

Rather, would to God the course of action here suggested might be fairly pursued! Would to God that the happy consequences which would result from the principles we have recommended be realized, and, above all, that the influence of true religion could be extensively diffused!

It is the best which one could make for one's country, by one who is deeply anxious for its welfare.

VII
Conclusion: Practical Hints for Real Christianity

We have attempted to trace the chief defects of the religious system of the bulk of professing Christians in this country.

We have pointed out their low idea of the importance of Christianity in general. We have seen their inadequate conceptions of all its leading doctrines and the effect of relaxing the strictness of its morality. Above all, we have discussed their fundamental misunderstanding of its genius and original nature.

Therefore do not consider the difference between them and true believers a trifling one, as if it were merely a matter of form and opinion. The issue is the very heart of religion. The difference is of the utmost seriousness. We must speak out.

Their Christianity is not Christianity.

It lacks the radical principle of true Christianity. It is defective in all the major constituents. Let them then no longer be deceived. Turn in humble prayer to the Source of all wisdom that He would enlighten their understanding and clear their hearts from prejudice. Let them seriously examine, by the Scriptures, their real belief and permitted practice. Then they will become aware of how shallow their scanty system is.

I. Practical Hints to Avoid Self-Deception

Proneness to
think too favor-
ably of oneself

Should any feel themselves disposed to the important duty of self-examination, let me warn such of our natural proneness to think too favorably of ourselves. Selfishness is one of the principal fruits of the corruption of human nature. It is obvious that selfishness disposes us to overrate our good qualities, and to overlook or excuse our defects. Admitting the corruption of human nature, we know we need to make allowance for the effects of selfishness.

Another effect of the corruption of human nature is the clouding of our moral sight, and the blunting of our moral sensitivity. This, too, we must allow for its effect upon us. There is little doubt that the perfect purity of the Supreme Being makes Him see in us stains—far more in number and deeper in dye—than we ourselves can discover.

Then we should not forget another awful consideration. For we tend to see only those things which we have recently fallen into, and overlook wrongs committed a while back. If recent, we will have deep remorse for such sins or vices. But after a few months or years, they leave but very faint traces in our recollection.

Now to God, we must believe there is no past or future. Whatever could be, and whatever has been, both are retained by him in present and unvarying contemplation. It may well humble us then, in the sight of "He who is of purer eyes than to behold evil" (Habakkuk 1:13), to remember the need of repentance.

Without true repentance and a lively faith, we shall all appear in lives clothed with our sins, sins in all their depth of coloring and with all the aggravations which we can no longer particularly remember. Yet we know they once filled us with shame and confusion of face. The writer is particularly anxious to enforce this reflection, because in his own experience, he has found nothing so effective in producing within his own soul the deepest self-humiliation.

We should also note other sources of self-deception: for example, the false estimates we form of our religion and moral character. The favorable opinions others may have of us may *mislead* many of us. Many also, it is to be feared, mistake a hot zeal for orthodoxy with a wholehearted acceptance of the great truths of the Gospel.

Almost all of us, at one time or another, are also misled more or less by confusing the suggestions of our understanding with the impulses of the will. So we confuse the assent which our judgment may give to religious and moral truths with a hearty belief and approval of them.

Another frequent source of self-deception is to see certain vices, as well as certain good and amiable qualities, as naturally belonging to particular periods and conditions of life. If we would really see our moral character as it truly is, we ought to examine ourselves with reference to that particular "sin which does so easily beset us" (Hebrews 12:1). We should not fix our attention on some other sin to which we are not nearly so liable. Likewise, we should not over-exaggerate the value of some good and amiable quality which naturally belongs to our culture and age. Rather we should look for some less uncertain sign of a real intrinsic principle of virtue.

But we are very prone to reverse these roles of judgment. We are apt to excuse "the besetting sin" and take credit for our exemption from others instead. On the other hand, we exaggerate the esteem of our good qualities of character which come naturally to us. So we do not think it necessary to probe deeper to find out what are the essential needs of our moral character.

Such smugness leaves us undisturbed, except when some great transgression we have committed shocks us. Instead, we should be looking for the positive marks of the true Christian, as laid down in the Holy Scripture.

But the source of self-deception we should first point out is this: a disposition to consider the relinquishment of any particular vice as an actual victory over the vice itself. In fact we only forsake it because we have left the period or condition of life to which that vice belongs. Probably we have substituted another one on entering a new period or condition of life. We thus mistake such changes in our worldly circumstances for a thorough reformation.

Youth   To apply this principle most practically we will take the case of young people. The youth of one sex may indulge occasionally in licentious excesses. Those of the other may be given over to vanity and pleasure. Provided they are sweet-tempered, and open, and not disobedient to their parents and superiors, the former are deemed *good-hearted* young men, and the latter *innocent* young women.

Now those who love these youths best have no concern about their spiritual interests. No one doubts they will become more religious as they advance in life. Still more, no one thinks of them being under divine displeasure. Nor indeed does anyone think of their lives as being in danger and their future destiny threatened.

Middle Age   So they grow older and marry. The same licentiousness which was formerly considered in them as a venial frailty is assumed to be past. "They have sown their wild oats; they must now reform and be regular." Likewise, we deem the former vanity and frivolous amusements to have disappeared with the matron.

If they are kind both in their conjugal and parental relation, tolerably regular and decent to others, then they pass for "mighty good sort of people." Their hearts, however, are perhaps not any more set supremely on the great work of salvation than they have been. Instead, their chief bent is on increasing their fortunes or raising their families.

Meanwhile they congratulate themselves on having removed their vices, which they are no longer strangely tempted to commit.

Old Age   At length, old age has made its advances. Now, if ever, we would expect it would be high time to make eternal things the great object of attention. No such thing! It is now required of them to be good-natured and indulgent to the frailties and follies of youth, remembering that when they were young they gave themselves up to the same practices.

How opposite this is to that dread of sin which is the sure characteristic of the true Christian. Such a dread causes him to look back upon the vices of his own youthful days with shame and sorrow. Then instead of conceding to young people to be wild and thoughtless—a privilege of their age and circumstances(!)—he is prompted to warn them against what has proved to him to be a matter of such bitter reflection.

Thus throughout the whole of life, we devise some means or other for stifling the voice of conscience. "We cry peace, when there is no peace!" (Jeremiah 6:14). So we find that complacency for ourselves and others. Yet that complacency should only proceed from the conscientiousness of being reconciled to God and seeking a humble hope of possessing His favor.

I know that many will term these sentiments uncharitable. I am not deterred by such a judgment.

Is this judgment uncharitable?

It is time to have done with such senseless cant of charity which insults true understanding and stifles real concern for the welfare of our fellow beings. What matter of keen remorse and of bitter reproaches they store up for their future torment! What miserable dupes they are of such misguided charity, when they have been charged to watch over the eternal interests of their children of relations! Why be lulled asleep by such shallow reasonings? Why be led into a dereliction of your important duty by the mere fear of bringing on a momentary pain!

True charity is wakeful, fervent, full of concern, full of good offices, not so easily satisfied, not so ready to believe that everything is going well as a matter of course. Rather, it is jealous of mischief, likely to suspect danger, and prompt to extend relief. That wretched quality by which the sacred name of charity is now so generally and so falsely usurped is none other than indifference.

Innocent young women! Good-hearted young men! Wherein does this *goodness of heart* and the *innocence* appear? Remember that we are fallen creatures, born in sin, and naturally depraved. Christianity recognizes no inno-

Christianity recognizes no innocence in a fallen world.

cence or goodness of heart but in the remission of sin, and in the effects of the operation of divine grace.

Do we find in these young persons the behaviors which the Scriptures lay down as the only satisfactory evidences of a safe state? Do we not, on the other hand, discover the specific marks of a state of alienation from God?

Can the blindest partiality persuade itself that they are loving and striving "to love God with all their hearts, and souls, and might"? (Deuteronomy 6:5). Are they "seeking first the kingdom of God and His righteousness"? (Matthew 6:33). Are they "working out their salvation with fear and trembling"? (Philippians 2:12). Are they "clothed with humility"? (1 Peter 5:5).

Are they not, on the contrary, entirely given up to self-indulgence? Are they not at least "lovers of pleasure more than lovers of God"? (2 Timohty 3:4). Are not the youth often actually committing sins (and still more often wishing for the opportunity to commit those sins) of which the Scripture says expressly, "that they which do such things shall not inherit the kingdom of God"? (Galatians 5:21).

True reform   Then when the first flush of youthful warmth is over, what is their boasted reformation? They may be decent, sober, useful, and respectable as members of the community, or amiable in their relations in domestic life. But is this the change of which the Scripture speaks?

Hear the expressions which Scripture states, and judge yourselves: "Except a man be born again, he cannot enter into the Kingdom of God" (John 3:5). "The old man is corrupt according to the deceitful lusts" (Ephesians 4:22). This expression is but too descriptive of the vain delusions of youthful pleasure seeking, and of the false dreams of happiness which it inspires. But the "new man" is awakened from this false state of happiness. He is "renewed in knowledge after the image of Him that created him" (Colossians 3:10). "He is created after God in righteousness and true holiness" (Ephesians 4:24).

Life is a state of probation.   Life is a state of probation. Probation implies resisting appetites which we naturally desire to gratify, in obedience to the dictates of true religion. Young people are not tempted to be churlish, selfish, or covetous; but they are tempted to be thoughtless and indulgent, "lovers of pleasure rather then lovers of God."

People in middle age are not so strongly tempted to be thoughtless, idle, and licentious. Happily settled in domestic life, they are freer from these tendencies. The restraints of family connections and a sense of the decencies of the married state help them in this regard.

Their probation is of another kind. Rather they are tempted to be supremely engrossed by worldly cares, by family interests, by professional objectives, and by the pursuit of wealth and ambition. Thus occupied they are tempted to "mind earthly rather than heavenly things" (John 3:12), to forget "the one thing needful" (Luke 10:42), to "set their affections" on temporal rather than on eternal concerns. They tend to take up with "a form of godliness" (2 Timothy 3:5) instead of seeking to experience the power thereof.

The foundations of this nominal religion are thus laid in forgetfulness, if not in ignorance, of the distinctive doctrines of Christianity. These are ready-made Christians who, we have already discovered, consider Christianity as a geographical term that is properly applicable to all who have been born and educated in a country where Christianity is professed. They do not see it as indicating a renewed nature. Nor do they see it as expressive of a distinctive character, with its appropriate desires and aversions, hopes and fears, joys and sorrows.

To people of this description, the solemn admonition of Christ is addressed: "I know thy works; that thou hast a name, that thou livest, and art dead. Be watchful and strengthen the things that remain, that are ready to die; for I have not found thy works perfect before God" (Revelation 3:1, 2).

Anyone disposed to listen to this solemn warning, who is awakened from his dreaming of false security, and disposed to be not *almost* but *altogether* a Christian—let him not stifle "the working of the divine Spirit." Let him be

Solemn warning to the indifferent and careless

drawn from this "broad" and crowded "road of destruction," into the "narrow" and thinly peopled "path that leadeth to life." Let him retire from the multitude. Let him enter into his closet and on his bended knees rely on his meditation to implore for Christ's sake that God would "take away from him the heart of stone, and give him a heart of flesh." Let him pray that the Father of light would open his eyes to his true condition, and clear his heart from the clouds of prejudice, and chase away the deceitful medium of self-love.

Then let him carefully examine his past life and his present course of conduct. Let him compare himself with God's Word and consider how one might reasonably be expected to conduct himself—one to whom the Holy Scriptures have always been opened and who is used to acknowledging them as the revelation of God's will as Creator and Governor and Supreme Benefactor. Let him then peruse the awful denunciations against impenitent sinners. Let him labor to become more and more deeply impressed with a sense of his own radical blindness and corruption.

Above all, let him steadily contemplate in all its relations this stupendous truth: the incarnation and crucifixion of the only begotten Son of God, and the message of mercy proclaimed from the cross to repenting sinners. "Be ye reconciled to God" (2 Corinthians 5:20). "Believe on the Lord Jesus Christ, and thou shalt be saved" (Acts 16:31).

When he estimates fairly the guilt of sin by the costly sacrifice of Jesus' death, and the worth of his own soul by the price that was paid for its redemption—then he will have such mixed emotions of guilt, fear, and shame. When he reflects on the amazing love and pity of Christ, and the cold and formal acknowledgments with which he has responded, then he may well have remorse and sorrow. When he thinks how he has trifled with the gracious invitation of his Redeemer, he may well strike his breast and cry out, "God be merciful to me a sinner" (Luke 18:13).

Yet to "the weary and heavy-laden," Christ still offers

rest; and to them who thirst, he gives the water of life. To them who are bound by "the chain of their sins," He gives deliverance. Cast yourselves then on His undeserved mercy. He is full of love and will not spurn you from His footstool. Surrender yourselves into his hands and solemnly resolve through His grace to dedicate henceforth all your faculties and powers to His service.

It is yours now "to work out your own salvation with fear and trembling," relying on the fidelity of Him who has promised to "work out in you both to will and to do of His good pleasure" (Philippians 2:13). Always look to Him for help. Your only safety consists in a deep and permanent sense of your own weakness; in a firm reliance on His strength. If you "give all diligence," His power is around for your protection; He pledges His truth for your security. "Faithful is He that hath promised" (Hebrews 10:23), so "be ye faithful unto death, and He will give you a crown of life" (Revelation 2:10). "He that endureth to the end, the same shall be saved" (Matthew 10:22).

In such a world as this, in such a state of society as ours, and especially in the higher walks of life, you must be prepared to meet with many difficulties. Arm yourselves, therefore, in the first place with a determined resolution not to rate human esteem beyond its true value. Do not dread the charge of being odd when it is necessary to incur it. Rather retain the vision in your conduct of seeking "the honor which cometh from God" (John 5:44). You cannot advance a single step until you are in some degree possessed of this comparative indifference to the favor of men.

Continue to be always aware of your own radical corruption and habitual weakness. Indeed, if you let God really open your eyes, and truly soften your heart, you will become daily more and more aware of your own defects, wants, and weaknesses. If you "hunger and thirst after righteousness," you will desire increasingly to purify yourself, even as God is pure.

This is the solution which seems such a strange paradox to the man of the world. In proportion as a Christian

Humility is the vital principle of Christianity.

grows in grace, so he grows in humility. Humility is indeed the principle first and last of Christianity. By this principle it lives and thrives. As humility grows or declines, so Christianity must flourish or decay.

Humility first disposes the sinner to have deep self-humiliation to accept the offers of the Gospel. During the whole of his progress, this is the very ground and basis of his feelings and conduct—in relation to God, to his fellow man, and to himself. When at length God translates him into the realms of glory, this principle shall still subsist in undiminished force: He "shall fall down and cast his crown before the Lamb, and ascribe blessing, and honor and glory, and power to Him that sitteth upon the throne and to the Lamb forever and ever" (Revelation 4:10, 5:13).

Practical benefits of humility

The practical benefits of the habitual lowliness of spirit are too numerous to require listing. It will lead you to dread the beginnings of sin and flee from its occasions, just as a man would shun an infectious disease. It will prevent a thousand difficulties and decide a thousand questions concerning worldly compromises. It will enable you to desire in your heart to act in all things with a single eye to the favor of God.

Thus the most ordinary actions of life will be elevated into religious exercises. It is a purifying, transmuting principle which realizes the fabled touch of the alchemist to change all into gold. It is the desire to please God in all things.

To so please God, it is also essential to guard against all the distractions of worldly cares. It needs the cultivation of heavenly-mindedness and a spirit of continual prayer. It requires you to watch incessantly over the workings of your own deceitful heart.

You need also to be active and useful. So let your precious time not be wasted "in shapeless idleness." This is an admonition which in our day persons of real piety even need. Never be satisfied with your present attainments, but "forgetting the things which are behind" labor still to "press forward" with undiminished energy, and to run the race that is set before you without weariness or intermission.

Above all, measure your progress by your experience of the love of God and its exercise before men. "God is love." This is the sacred principle which warms and enlightens the heavenly world, that blessed seat of God's visible presence. There it shines with unclouded radiance. Some scattered beams of it are graciously transmitted to us on earth, or we would have been benighted and lost in darkness and misery. But a larger portion of it is poured into the hearts of the servants of God, who are thus "renewed in the divine likeness." It is the principle of love which disposes them to yield themselves up without reserve to the service of Him "who bought them with the price of his own blood" (1 Corinthians 6:20).

The principle of God's love

In contrast, servile, base, and mercenary is the notion of Christian practice among the bulk of nominal Christians. They give no more than they dare not withhold. They abstain from nothing but what they must not practice. When you state to them the doubtful quality of any action, and the consequent obligation to refrain from it, they reply to you in the very spirit of Shylock, "they cannot find it in the bound."

In short, they know Christianity only as a system of restraints. It is robbed of every liberal and generous principle. It is rendered almost unfit for the social relationships of life, and only suited to the gloomy walls of a cloister, in which they would confine it.

But true Christians consider themselves as not satisfying some rigorous creditor, but as discharging a debt of gratitude. Accordingly theirs is not the stinted return of a constrained obedience, but the large and liberal measure of voluntary service.

This principle of the love of God enables the true Christian to be like the apostles: "rejoicing that they were counted worthy to suffer shame for the name of Jesus" (Acts 5:41). It also regulates the true Christian's choice of companions and friends, when he is at liberty to make an option. It fills him with the desire of promoting the temporal welfare of all around him, and still more with pity and love as he is anxious for their spiritual happiness. Indifference, then, to this principle is one of the surest signs of a low or declining state of true religion.

Forward look of the true Christian

Another principle of the true Christian is that he recognizes this world is not his resting place. Here to the very last, he must be a pilgrim and a stranger. He is a soldier, whose welfare ends only with life. He is ever struggling and combating with the powers of darkness, and the temptations of the world around him, and the still more dangerous hostilities of inward sinfulness.

Thus the perpetual struggles, trials, difficulties, and infirmities which checker the life of a Christian teach him to look forward to that promised day when he shall be completely delivered from the bondage of corruption. Then sorrow and sighing shall flee away. He anticipates that blessed future, where love shall reign without disturbance, and all shall be knit together in the bonds of indissoluble friendship, and all shall be united in the one harmonious song of praise to the Author of their blessedness. For the true Christian triumphs over the fear of death. Such, then, are the habitual feelings of the real believer.

II. Advice to Some Who Profess Their Full Assent to the Fundamental Doctrines of the Gospel

In a former chapter, we emphasized that the fundamental, practical error of the bulk of professing Christians today is to overlook or misconceive the way in which the Gospel has provided for: first, the renovation of our corrupted nature, and, second, the attainment of every Christian grace.

Scripture and experience both warrant that we need to prescribe hearty repentance and lively faith as the only foundation of all true holiness. Yet we must also guard against another practical mistake. Those who with penitent hearts have humbled themselves before the cross of Christ can be led to assume their work is now all done.

Pleading the merits of Christ as their only ground of pardon and acceptance with God, and resolved to bring forth the fruits of righteousness by the help of His Spirit, they may again fall into sin and need a fresh act of repentance.

There are many who satisfy themselves with what may be termed "general Christianity." They feel a general penitence and humiliation from a general sense of sinfulness and have general desires for holiness. Yet they neglect this vigilant and zealous care with which they should labor to destroy every particular form of corruption. Likewise, they are far from striving with perseverance, for the acquisition and improvement of every Christian grace.

Nor is it unusual for ministers—who preach the truths of the Gospel with fidelity, ability, and success—to be themselves also liable to the charge of dwelling altogether, in their instructions, within general religion. Instead of tracing and laying open all the secret motions of inward corruption, and instructing their hearers how best to conduct themselves in every distant phase of the Christian warfare, they generalize about it all. So we see little progress in their development of faith or in the reform of their plan of life. They will confess in general terms to be "miserable sinners." But it is an expression really of secret self-complacency.

Warning to ministers of the Gospel

We need to warn such persons that there is no shortcut to holiness. It must be the business of their whole lives to grow in grace and continually to add one virtue to another. It is as far as possible, "to go on towards perfection" (Hebrews 6:1). "He only that doeth righteousness is righteous" (1 John 3:7). Unless they bring forth "the fruit of the Spirit" (Galatians 5:22), they can have no sufficient evidence that they have actually received the Spirit of Christ, "without which they are none of His" (Romans 8:9). Unless, then, the root of the matter is not found in them, they are not adorning the doctrine of God, but disparaging and discrediting it.

No shortcut to holiness

The world does not see their secret humiliations nor

the exercises of their closets. But the world is acute in discerning practical weaknesses. If the world observes that they have the same eagerness in the pursuit of wealth and ambition, the same vain taste for pretentiousness and display, the same ungoverned tempers, which are found in the generality of mankind—then it will treat with contempt their pretenses to be superior in sanctity and indifferent to worldly things. Then such a soul will become hardened in its prejudices against the only way which God has provided for our escape of the wrath to come and our attainment in eternal happiness.

Let him, then, who would be indeed a Christian, watch over his ways and over his heart—with unceasing circumspection. Let him endeavor to learn both from the lives of godly men and devotional books—particularly from the lives of eminent Christians—the methods which they have actually found to be most effective for the conquest of every particular vice, and for the improvement in every aspect of holiness. [Here Wilberforce notes the lives of many that he has read, some now unknown, but others still well known such as Archbishop Robert Leighton, Matthew Hale, Philip Doddridge, Richard Baxter, John Wesley, Henry Martyn, and Colonel Gardiner, etc.]

Thus while he studies his own character and observes the more intimate workings of his own mind, he will acquire insights of the human heart in general. This will enable him to guard against all occasions of evil. Such a perspective will also tend, above all things, to promote the growth of humility and to maintain that sobriety of spirit and tenderness of conscience which are the characteristic marks of the true Christian. It is by this unceasing diligence—as the apostle declares it—that the servants of Christ make their calling sure. It is only thus that their labor will ultimately succeed. "So an entrance shall be ministered unto them abundantly, into the everlasting kingdom of our Lord and Savior Jesus Christ" (2 Peter 1:11).

III. A CHALLENGE TO UNBELIEVERS

Another class of men—an increasing class, it is to be feared, in this country—is that of absolute unbelievers. While this work is not properly concerned with them, we nevertheless pity their state. So the writer may be permitted to ask them one plain question. If Christianity is not true in their judgment, yet least should it not surely be entitled to a serious examination?

Men like Bacon, Milton, Locke, and Newton made full inquiry and deep consideration of Christianity. Such men, by the reading of their understanding, the extent of their knowledge, and the desire to combat existing prejudices, called forth the admiration of mankind. What, too, of those churchmen, some of whom are among the greatest names this country has ever known?

Can the skeptic in general say with truth that he has pursued an examination into all the evidences of revelation at all? Or has he at least with serious diligence looked into the importance of the subject? The fact is, such unbelief is not the result of sober inquiry or of deliberate preference. Rather it is the slow production of a careless and irreligious life, operating together with prejudices and erroneous conceptions about the leading doctrines and fundamental tenets of Christianity.

A typical case of such unbelief begins when young men are brought up as nominal Christians. Their parents take them to church as children and there they become acquainted with those passages of the Bible used in the service. If their parents still keep some of the old habits, they may even be taught the catechism.

The rise and growth of skepticism

But they go off into the world, yield to youthful temptations, neglect to look at their Bible, and they do not develop their religious duties. They do not even try to reflect, study, or mature in the thoughts that they once might have had as children. They may even travel abroad, relax still further their religious habits, and tend to read only about those controversial issues of religion.

Attending church occasionally, these occasional incidents more often offend such youth than strengthen them. Perhaps they are tempted to be morally superior to those they think are superstitious. Or the poor examples of some professing Christians disgust them. Or else they stumble because of the absurdities of others who see they are equally ignorant to themselves. At any rate, they gradually begin to doubt the reality of Christianity. A confused sense of relief that it is all untrue settles within them. Impressions deepen, reinforced by fresh arguments. At length they are convinced of their doubts in a broad sweep over the whole realm of religion.

This may not be universally so, but it may be termed the natural history of skepticism. It is the experience of those who have watched the progress of unbelief in those they care about. It is confirmed by the written lines of some of the most eminent unbelievers. We find that they once gave a sort of implicit, inherited assent to the truth of Christianity and were considered believers.

How then did they become skeptics? Reason, thought, and inquiry have little to do with it. Having lived for many years careless and irreligious lives, they eventually matured in their faithlessness—not by force of irreligious strength but by lapse of time. This is generally the offspring of prejudice, and its success is the result of moral depravity. Unbelief is not so much the result of a studious and controversial age as it is one of moral decline. It disperses itself in proportion as the general morals decline. People embrace it with less apprehension when all around are doing the same thing.

This account of the secret but most common cause of much unbelief may justifiably extend to include all those who deny the fundamental doctrines of the Gospel.

Unitarianism a half-way state

A halfway house between nominal orthodoxy and total denial of Christianity is unitarianism. Some may stop there, but for others it is only a temporary halt. Then they make the pursuit into further unbelief.

Unitarian teachers by no means profess to free their followers from the unbending strictness of Christian morality. They prescribe the predominant importance of the love of God, and they seek a habitual spirit of devotion. But they are not distinguished by a superior purity of life, nor still less by that spirituality of mind which the Word of God prescribes to us. This state of mind is one of the surest tests of our experiencing the vital power of Christianity.

We can explain unitarianism as a faith of understanding, rather than one of the heart. It is produced by the confused intellectual difficulties and impossibilities in which orthodox Christianity seems to be involved. Even more so than the Deists, the Unitarians attack with strong arguments the fundamental doctrines of Christianity and then call upon men to abandon the positions they think they have abolished by their arguments. Truly they can cite perplexing difficulties and plausible objections against the most established truths. But is that a reason for abandoning them? If they proceed logically, they will find no rest for the sole of their foot and not stop short of atheism.

Besides those who openly reject revelation, there is an increasing class of half-believers who are found in various conditions. They see there is "something in it," but deny the fundamental truths of Christianity. So they take up a strange middle position of its qualified truth. Yet they do not see themselves as enlisted under the banners of unbelief. We should remind them that if they look into their Bibles, and they do not finally reject its authority, they will find no basis for their "middle-ground."

IV. BEING TRUE CHRISTIANS BECAUSE OF THE STATE OF OUR TIMES

To those who really deserve to be called true Christians, much has been said incidentally throughout this book. I have maintained that they are always most important members of the community. No sound or experienced politician would deny that. But we boldly assert that there never was a period when this was truer than of the present time. For wherever we look we see that religion and the standards of morals are everywhere declining, abroad more rapidly than in our own country.

However, at home the progress of irreligion and the decline in morals is enough to alarm every thoughtful person and to fill us with foreboding about the growth of evil. We can only depend upon true Christians to give some remedy against its decline. Zeal is required in the cause of religion and only they can feel it. Singleness of purpose, consistency of behavior, and perseverance in effort are needed. Only true Christians can provide these qualities.

True Christians take their faith seriously.

Let true Christians, with becoming earnestness, strive in all things to recommend their profession and to put to silence the vain scorn of ignorant objections. Let them boldly assert the cause of Christ in an age when so many who bear the name of Christian are ashamed of Him. Let them accept the duty to serve, if not actually to save, their country. Let them serve not by political interference, but by that sure and radical benefit of restoring the influence of true religion and of raising the standard of morality.

Let them be active, useful, and generous toward others. Let them show moderation and self-denial in themselves. Let them be ashamed of idleness. When blessed with wealth, let them withdraw from the competition of vanity and be modest, retiring from ostentation, and not be the slaves of fashion. Let them be moderate in all things. Let them cultivate a catholic spirit of general good will and of kindness toward others. Let them encourage men of real piety—wherever they may be found—and others to repress vice and revive and spread the influence of real Christianity. Let them pray earnestly for the renewal of its vitality.

Let them pray continually for their country at this time of national difficulty. We bear the marks only too plainly of a declining empire. Who can say how intercession before the Governor of the universe may avert for a while our ruin. It may appear before the eyes of the world foolishness for real Christians so to pray, yet we believe from Scripture that God will be disposed to favor the nation to which His servants belong.

Boldly I must confess that I believe the national difficulties we face result from the decline of religion and morality among us. I must confess equally boldly that my own solid hopes for the well-being of my country depend, not so much on her navies and armies, nor on the wisdom of her rulers, nor on the spirit of her people, as on the persuasion that she still contains many who love and obey the Gospel of Christ. I believe that their prayers may yet prevail.

So let the prayers of the Christian reader also be offered up for the success of this feeble endeavor in the service of true religion. For God can give effect to the weakest effort. The writer will feel most privileged if what he has written awakens the conscience of a single person and encourages him to more usefulness.

In so much of Europe, they have preferred a false philosophy before the lessons of revelation. Infidelity has lifted up her head without shame, and walks broadly in the daytime. Licentiousness and vice prevail without restraint.

May there be here at least a sanctuary, a land of true faith and piety, where we may still enjoy the blessings of Christianity. May there be here in this nation a place where the name of Christ is still honored and men may see the blessings of faith in Jesus. May the means of religious education and consolation once again be extended to surrounding countries and to the world at large.